SURRENDER!

THE LIFE-CHANGING POWER
OF DOING GOD'S WILL

SURRENDER!

THE LIFE-CHANGING POWER OF
DOING GOD'S WILL

FR. LARRY RICHARDS

Our Sunday Visitor Publishing Division
Our Sunday Visitor, Inc.
Huntington, IN 46750

Nihil Obstat:
Msgr. Michael Heintz, Ph.D.
Censor Librorum

Imprimatur:
✠ Kevin C. Rhoades
Bishop of Fort Wayne-South Bend
May 25, 2011

The *Nihil Obstat* and *Imprimatur* are declarations that a work is free from doctrinal or moral error. It is not implied that those who have granted the *Nihil Obstat* and *Imprimatur* agree with the contents, opinions, or statements expressed.

CONTENTS

PREFACE

Surrender! Don't you just hate that word? I know that I do, especially when it is used to mean being conquered, defeated, or filled with despair. Relax. This is NOT what I mean when I use the word! In this book, surrender means abandoning our lives to the One who loves us and gave His life for us. I use this word as Jesus does. He says to us there is *no greater love than this, to lay down one's life for His friends* (see John 15:13). Jesus is our model for surrender. He gives everything to us, and so we respond in like manner. He starts it and we respond.

Once I was speaking to about 300 men at a church in Mobile, Alabama, at 6:30 in the morning. They had come to hear me speak on male spirituality. As I always do, I spoke about the need to surrender ourselves to God before we can do anything else. After my talk, I fielded questions, and one of the men asked, "Father why don't we hear about the need of total surrender more often?" It was one of the few times I did not really know how to answer. I said that I think most people are scared to death of the whole concept of surrender. They are afraid it will cost them everything to surrender.

And it will!

When we decide that we want to live life God's way instead of our way, we are going to have to give up our way and trust that God's way is better. I have often quoted my spiritual director, who has said to me repeatedly that the theme song of those in hell is, "I did it my way." No intention to hurt Frank Sinatra fans, but this is so true! We so often think that we know best, and that if God and the world did things our way then everything would work out okay. Talk about a God complex!

We cannot even take our next breath without God saying that it is okay. We are very dependent people. It is that simple. God can take your breath away right now, and you are done. So we need to learn to trust Him. We need to know that He loves us and that He wants us to be happy more than we want to be happy.

Remember the question in the old *Baltimore Catechism,* "Why did God make me?" The answer is "to know Him, to love Him and to serve Him in this world, so we can be happy forever in heaven." God loves us more than we could ever begin to love ourselves. Do you believe that? Do you live that?

This is the purpose of this book: to give you the practical steps to daily surrender your life to God and His will. It is not about giving up your free will and becoming a cult member. It is about your putting your will freely under the will of your heavenly Father God. Jesus showed us how to do this. Throughout His life He said, *The world must know that I love the Father and do everything to please Him* (see John 14:31).

This surrender is not a passive "giving up," like the surrender of Islam. The word "Islam" means surrender, but it is usually inactive — if God wills it, so be it. We find the kind of surrender I am talking about in the example of Mary when she says, "Let it be done to me" — *Fiat!* Hers was not a passive acceptance of whatever might happen. Mary's *fiat* was an active desire to seek out and live God's will. It was a complete willingness to do everything that God called her to do. This is what we must do, too. When Mary said "Yes" to God's will, she brought salvation to the world. The same thing happens to us when we say "Yes" to His will. We become instruments of salvation for our families, the world, and ourselves.

To surrender is to love. This is not surrender of fear or of self-interest, but a response to a loving invitation in the journey to eternal life. It is the surrender that is life-giving. It is the ultimate surrender, and the only one that really matters. We are going to explore this loving surrender in our seeking to know and live God's will.

When you surrender your will daily to the will of Our Father, then you will discover the joy of totally giving yourself to the One who has totally given Himself to you. You will enter into the relationship of trust and love with the God of the Universe. You don't have to be afraid; you just need to trust, for He promises that He will never leave you or forsake you. He promises that He will lead you and guild you. He promises that He will give you His peace.

Are you ready?

Get excited! God has great plans for you.

Let's start to surrender.

CHAPTER 1

Surrender and Go to Heaven!

"[God] chose us in him, before the foundation of the world, to be holy and without blemish before him. In love he destined us for adoption to himself." (Ephesians 1:4, NAB)

God wants you in heaven. Isn't that a great thought? God's will for you is not to go to purgatory. God's will is not for you to go to hell. God's will for you is to go to heaven. The ultimate will of God is for you and me to go to heaven and be with Him forever. God is not "out to get us." He wants to love us forever and He wants us to live with Him and enjoy eternal life! This is what God desires. That is why He created you and me. Once we realize this is the ultimate will of God, everything flows from this reality.

We read in 2 Timothy 1:9, *God has saved us and has called us to a holy life, not because of any merit of ours but according to His own design — the Grace held out to us in Christ Jesus before the world began.* To be saved means to go to heaven ultimately. This is a general plan for everybody.

"There is only one tragedy — not to be a saint," Leon Bloy states in his book *The Woman Who Was Poor.* I put it this way: you have a choice — become a saint or go to hell. This is where we need to begin our discussion on knowing and living God's will in our lives. You and I were created for heaven. It is the overall will of God that you and I live forever with Him. We need to do everything in our power to cooperate with His will.

You have a choice: become a saint or go to hell. (I have said this twice to hammer in my point — is it working?)

I once gave a talk to about 1,000 youths in Halifax, Nova Scotia. I was the first speaker for the weekend. At the opening Mass about six bishops behind me were concelebrating. As I got up to preach the homily, I looked at those 1,000 youth and said to them, "Ladies and gentlemen, you have two choices. Either you become a saint or you go to hell!" Well, you should have seen the look on those bishops' faces! They were not very happy with me at first, but they relaxed as I continued and helped the youths to see that we are all called to holiness. It needs to be the same with you who are reading this book. God wants you to be holy, and I will do anything to make sure that He gets your attention!

Right now you need to make a decision to desire God's will in your life. God does everything in His power to save us and get us to heaven. In fact, He gave up His only Son for each of us. He also gave you and me the gift of free will so that we can choose to be with Him or not. This choice is up to us and it is an eternal one. We see in Ephesians 1:4–6 that *God chose us in His Son before the world began to be holy and blameless in His sight and full of love.* Therefore, before we start to talk about the particular will of God for our lives, we need to look at the general will of God. As we have stressed, the general will of God is that we are saved, that we go to heaven, and that we become holy. Everything else is going to be secondary.

In 1 Timothy 2:4 God tells us, *He wants all people to be saved and come to the knowledge of His truth.* God wants everyone in heaven with Him, and that includes you.

God does everything in His power to save us! Let that sink in. God does everything in His power to save you!

Who messes that up? We do because we go against the will of God. We don't cooperate with God's will for our lives. You see, when we go against the will of God, we kill ourselves spiritually. It's an act of self-destruction. Both Adam and Eve were the first to do that. When they decided they were going to do it their way instead of God's way and disobeyed God, death came to them, suffering came to them, and to the entire world. When we go against the will of God, we kill ourselves. It's an act of self-destruction. Eve was the first to do that. When we surrender to God's plan for us, we're on the road to eternal life. God does everything if you will; He creates us, and then He dies for us. He pays the price for our salvation.

Because God loves us, we do not have to be afraid. We talk about the fear of the Lord as being the beginning of wisdom, but the fear of God isn't terror; it's awe.

Have you ever seen the most beautiful sunrise and stood there in absolute awe, humbled to nothingness? Or perhaps you've seen the birth of a child, and you felt like, "Whoa!" That's the fear of the Lord. It is the realization "You are God and I am not, and I am in awe of You!"

Jesus was the best example of this. He did not live being afraid of His Father. He went around in awe of His Father; in love with His Father; knowing that in His humanity His Father was greater than Him; obeying His Father in all things because of trust. He was not walking around afraid all the time. When you and I walk around afraid of God, that is an awful thing and it is not what God wants.

Remember that John says, *When there is fear, love has not yet been perfected* (see 1 John 4:18). When we are in love, it casts away all fear. So when we are talking about God, we're talking about wanting to be one with Him. We are talking about our trusting Him, and trusting that He loves us.

After reading my book *Be a Man*, people often ask me what the most important chapter is (and they often think I'm going to say Chapter 3 because it is on Repentance — not even close!). I always say that it is Chapter 2 — "Be a Man Who Knows that He Is God's Beloved Son." Before you can repent, before you can do any other steps, you have to know you are loved by God! You have to know you are the beloved of your Father in heaven.

As children, we sometimes think that every time we mess up God says, "Ha ha ha. I've got you now. I've been waiting for this (whack)." Moreover, we think, "Yes, I deserve it." That is our image of God. What a bad image!

Let's say you find your child trying to walk and he falls. Do you say, "Come here (whack). You stupid little child! You should be walking by now. Get up and walk." You do not do that, do you? (If you do, you are a sick human being.) Neither does God. When we fall, God is still pleased with us for wanting to do His will. If we are striving to do His will, He is pleased because He loves us.

We are His beloved.

You are His beloved.

That doesn't mean we don't have to change. You have to change, oh yeah. You're still selfish. So am I. Does that have to change? Absolutely. Can I still go to hell? Absolutely, if I am doing things my way. I've got to be afraid because this God who loves me will give me what I want at the end, and if what I want isn't Him I'm going to hell.

But that's not what God wants. Is that what we really want? The teaching of the Church has always been clear — fear of hell is enough to get you to heaven. But we should go far beyond that. For example, if your kids are just listening to you because they are afraid of you, you have failed as a parent. My dogs do everything I tell them because they are afraid I'll punish them, but my dogs aren't my kids. There is a big difference between a dog and a child. And so it must be with us because we are God's children.

We do not have to be afraid. God loves us more than we could ever even begin to love ourselves. We just need to surrender and to trust. Sometimes this is hard because there can seem to be so much darkness around us, but we are called to trust our Father as if we were caught in the third floor of a burning house. We cannot get out, and then we hear our Father's voice from below the smoke crying out, "Do not be afraid. I am here. Jump and I will catch you!" To be saved we must jump or die. We need to do everything that it takes in our own lives to accept the fact that God sent His only Son to die for us and all we have to do is surrender!

Now before we go on much further, let me make one thing clear — we are not talking about salvation as if it comes only from what we do. It comes by cooperating with what Jesus did for us on the cross. We are saved by grace. Period. BUT, we've got to cooperate with that grace.

When we stand before God and He asks, "Why should I let you into heaven?" the only answer is, "Because Jesus Christ died for my sins." God will respond to you, "Prove it," and then you will have to show Him the way you lived. But again, salvation comes from the grace of God. That is why all Christians, Catholics and Protestants alike, have as our theme song, "Amazing Grace" with the telling words, "How sweet the sound, that saved a wretch like me." We wretches will become saints if we keep cooperating with God since we are all saved by grace.

When we surrender to God, then we can grow in His holiness. Holiness is who we are — not what we do. This is very important to understand. We are holy because of our baptism, because we have been set apart for God, because God dwells in us, not because we are good people. This is found, of course, in the teaching of the Church. As I already stated in the preface, the old *Baltimore Catechism* taught us in Number 1, Lesson 1, Question 6:

Question: Why did God make you?

Answer: God made me to know Him, to love Him, and to serve Him in this world, and to be happy with Him forever in heaven.

God created us to be happy forever in heaven! That is the meaning of Life!

But what does it mean to know God? First of all, to know God doesn't mean knowing about God. It's having an intimate relationship with God. You can know a lot about God, but that does not mean that you know God.

Let me give you an example. I have almost 160 CDs available, and all my talks are on iTunes. People who have listened to my material often come up to me and say, "Oh Father, I know everything about you." And I say, "Oh you know everything about me, but you don't know me." They respond, "Well, sure I do Father. I know all your talks and I've listened to every one of your talks." (You poor person. That'll get you out of purgatory just by itself.) And I'll say again, "But, you don't know me." They know what I say, but they don't know me, the real person.

I taught at Cathedral Prep, an all-boys Catholic high school in Erie, Pennsylvania, for eight years and the kids there used to ask, "Father, how come you always sound so nice on those CDs?" (They said that because they knew I'm not always nice.) Everywhere I go, people come up to me at parish missions and tell me, "Oh Father, your parish is so blessed to have you." I say, "You think so? Just ask one of my parishioners. They'll tell you how blessed they are." Why do I say this? Because I am not this perfect person. I'm not even close to one.

The point is that people who listen to my tapes or attend my missions have all these images of me, but they don't know me. The people in the parish know me. For good or for bad. (It's always amazing — the people who love you love you in spite of all your bad qualities. The people who hate you, hate you in spite of all your good qualities. It all depends on what you decide to look at. We all have good. We all have bad. Every one of us. And so, we have to grow in our good.)

That is the point I want to make about knowing about me and knowing me. To know about me is much different than knowing me. To know God is much different than knowing about God. You can know all the commandments; you can obey every rule; learn all the things in the *Catechism*, but the question is, "Do you have this relationship with God? Do you spend time with God?" In the end, that is the only thing that matters.

It's a relationship that's a two-way street. It is an experiential knowledge. Pope Benedict calls it a "friendship with Jesus." When Pope Benedict was speaking in the United States, in almost every talk he gave, he called us to have this "friendship with Jesus." In John 15:14, Jesus tells us, *You are my friends.* He is our friend, but are we His friend? If I were to ask you for your top ten list of friends, would Jesus Christ even make your list?

Holiness flows out of this friendship with Jesus Christ. He is our friend; we are His friend. Spending time with Him is how we grow in friendship. This is true for our relationship with God — to know Him we have to spend quality time with Him. This takes time and commitment, but it's not an option.

We need to develop in holiness. We know that babies do not start walking as soon as they come out of their mothers, so neither do we mature in the holiness all at once. It is a progression. It is a lifelong process. The important thing is that we need to want this process to be ongoing in our lives and to desire it as God desires it!

How great is it that our God wants only what is best for us? That He desires us to live with Him forever? That He wants us to be just like Him?

The general will of God is that we are saved, we become holy, and then we go to heaven. This means you become a saint. What a great plan!

To be a saint, by definition, means that you make it to heaven. I love that Blessed John Paul the Great declared more than a thousand saints. He did not make them, but he brought them forth in canonization or beatification. More than thousand people — married people, single people, priests, and religious! Real people! John Paul II canonized more saints and beatified more blesseds than any other pope in the history of the Church. He wanted to show that real people could become saints. So the first thing you've got to ask yourself on the way to holiness is, "Do I want to be a saint? Is that my goal?"

It is the goal of all the saints. From a very young age, St. Thérèse the Little Flower had a great desire for sanctity; she wanted to be a saint. It has to be our goal, too. However, this cannot be the end in itself. The main reason we want to become saints is to please the Father and to be with Him forever, not just to avoid hell and be happy forever.

I was watching TV once and heard a man in an interview say, "I want to be a saint, but I don't just want to be any saint. I want to be a great saint." Now I am sure that he was pure of heart and did not realize how his statement came off, but there can be a lot of self-interest in that statement. He wanted to be one of the "top" saints in heaven. He didn't want to be a lowly saint. Why do you want to be a saint? Do you want to be a saint so people will pray to you? Come on, that's self-interest. Do you want to be a saint so you can be great? That is self-interest, too. Or do you want to be a saint simply because you want to be with God, to love Him forever?

Sanctity or holiness is a by-product of love. It is not an end in itself. People who stay so focused on their own lives, always concentrating on whether they did something good or bad, drive me crazy! I want to cry, "Get over yourself! It isn't about you."

If I need to say that a billion times, I will!

Learn it. Know it. Live it.

Christianity isn't the focus on self. It is the forgetfulness of self! It's a surrender of love to the Father. When you and I fully surrender, that's when we become holier. When you and I focus on our own little acts of holiness or acts of sins, we become Pharisees. Remember, the Pharisees did everything right. They not only didn't break the Ten Commandments, they didn't break the 700 commandments of Leviticus. But they could still be in hell. Why? They didn't break any commandments. It is because it was all about them; how they were going to "earn" holiness; how they were going to "earn" heaven. That is a lie, people. That is not grace. That is not love. That is not God's will.

So think about the question, "Why do I want to go to heaven?" Is it because I am afraid of hell? Again, if that is the only reason, it's an act of selfishness. It is saying, "I don't want to go to hell, so I guess I'll go to heaven." If that is the case, then our whole life of Christianity is focusing on that reality.

Again, as I look at my own life, I realize I'm a very imperfect person (in case anybody doesn't know that yet), and there are a lot of imperfect people around me. But the reality is that God is calling us to become people of love, people who are real.

We need to be clear that you do not need to be a priest, nun, religious sister, brother, or even a deacon to be a saint. In fact, sometimes a religious vocation can keep a person from holiness if they are not seeking God's will in their daily lives, or take their vocation as a job instead of a response of doing our Father's will because they love Him and want to make Him happy. Remember, Jesus said, *The world must know that I love the Father and that I do everything to please Him!* (see John 14:31). How about you? Does the world know that you love the Father? Can people see that you love the Father and seek only to please Him, or do they see that you love yourself and do only what pleases you?

Incidentally, do you know you can have sex every day with your spouse and still become a saint? I know that sounds shocking, but it is true! Remember, holiness is a by-product of love. So if you're doing the will of God in your life and living a life of love, whether you're married (having sex) or single, a priest or a religious (not having sex) — then you're being holy. You are doing what God created you to do.

Blessed Pope John Paul II made sure that the saints he brought forth for canonization were young and old, mothers and fathers, poor and wealthy, priests, sisters, and singles. He did this because he wanted to remind us that the call to holiness is for everyone and that we need to desire this and cooperate with this great calling every day!

You can be holy and still be real. This is a very big thing for me — to be real. Sometimes people think that they have to act all holy and use "holy talk" to be a saint. Most of the time, I think it is the exact opposite. Look at St. Padre Pio. In spite of having the stigmata, the ability to bilocate, and the ability to read souls, he had good moods and bad moods. When he was told that Rome had barred him from hearing confessions and saying Mass in public for a while, he went to his room and cried.

I love to know that St. Padre and all the saints had to go to confession for their sins! There were only two people who never committed sin — Jesus and Mary — and we aren't them! This should give us great hope that, despite our moodiness, sins, good days and bad days, God is still calling us to be His saints. It is HE who makes us holy, not us who make ourselves holy.

The key to holiness is daily surrender in our prayer. We need to have a longing for God's will in spite of our sinfulness. In my book *Be a Man*, I used King David as an example of a man from whom we can get hope. He was a murderer, a rapist, an adulterer — basically, he was a selfish person, but he was also "A man after God's own heart!" Not because he was a murderer, a rapist, and adulterer, but because he surrendered to God and God made him holy. God can do the same with you if you let Him. You need to be a person after God's own heart and seek His will more than you seek your next breath. Ask for this grace; God is so generous with His grace to those who ask! He wants you to be a saint in heaven more than you want to be! What a thought!

We can also gain hope from someone such as Blessed Pier Giorgio Frassati. He was a young man who liked sports, having fun with his friends, rock climbing, smoking pipes, as well as spending time with Jesus in the Blessed Sacrament, taking care of the poor, and seeking God's will above all. As far as we know, he never desired to be a priest, but wanted to be married. Throughout his life, he would defend the faith strongly and was not ashamed of Jesus. He lived a full and fast life and died at the age of twenty-four. John Paul beatified him on May 20, 1990. Pier Giorgio is an inspiration to many young adults who want to be holy and still want to be married or live a single life outside of the religious life.

We have already reflected on St. Thérèse of Lisieux, but now let us focus on her mother, Blessed Zélie Martin and her father, Blessed Louis Martin, who were beatified in October 19, 2008. These are great examples of people who were regular people. They had sex and God still called them to be saints. Blessed Zélie and Louise were very real people who struggled with all the things that we struggle with. They persevered through many tragedies, but focused on God instead of themselves.

Blessed Zélie Martin reflected on the deaths of some of her children in these words, "When I closed the eyes of my dear children and prepared them for burial, I was indeed grief-stricken, but, thanks to God's grace, I have always been resigned to His will. I do not regret the pains and sacrifices I underwent for them." She went on to say that she "doesn't understand people who say, 'You'd have been better not to have gone though all of that,'" adding, "They're enjoying heaven now. Moreover, I have not lost them always. Life is short, and I shall find my little ones again in heaven."[1]

Can you imagine losing your child, or children as she did, and going through that suffering and realizing that even this, one of the deepest darknesses you could ever encounter in life, is nothing because one day you will be with your child forever in heaven? We go through all our struggles, all our sufferings, all our doubts, and yet we still know that you and I are called to be holy, called to be saints. In the midst of the darkness, we are called to be light.

It was from her parents that St. Thérèse learned how to be a saint. Those of you who are parents, are your children learning how to be a saint from you? You see, you are not only called to be a saint but you are called to be "saint makers" with your children! You got a lot of work to do! Aren't you excited?

Again you may not be called to be a virgin or a martyr, a priest or a bishop, or a missionary, but you are called to be a saint — an extraordinary saint, a saint who will do God's will. Is this what you want? That is the real question here.

Before you started reading this book, if I sat you down and handed you a piece of paper and asked you to write down ten goals, would holiness have ever even made it on the list? Is holiness one of your goals in your life? It sure should be. We read in Hebrews 12:14 that we are to *Strive for that holiness, without which you will not see the Lord.* Ouch. Read that again. Let it sink in. This is what God says you must do to see Him — strive for holiness.

Most people believe that they are good persons. If I were to ask you, "Are you a good person?" I'll bet most of you would say, "Yes, Father, I'm a pretty good person. I am nice to others. I don't steal, or do any other real bad things. So I guess, yes, I'm a pretty good person." If I were then to then ask you, "Are you a holy person?" I'll bet you would say, "No, no, I'm not a holy person, Father." And I'd say, "Well you darn well better be. God created you to be holy. That's who you are."

We've got to grow in this holiness. As I said before, you did not come out of your mother walking. No, it took time. After you were born, it took a while to start crawling, and eventually you tried walking. You fell a lot before you could finally walk. It's the same in the spiritual life. Holiness is something we grow into.

When Paul was writing many of his letters, he called the whole church the "Saints of God." We are the Saints of God. We are not saints who have already made it, but we are saints in process. I love the saying that "The Church isn't a museum of saints. It's a hospital for sinners." We can add, "Sinners on their way to becoming saints." That is the point. We are all in different stages of this journey but we've all got to be on the journey. This is what God is calling you and me to do. He wants us to be with Him forever, and the way we do this is to grow into the holiness that God is calling us to.

But, as I've said, it's our choice. Even though God wants us all to be in heaven, He still created hell. Why is this? Because if there is no choice, there is no love. Since God is a God of love, there must be a choice.

Ultimately, as I have preached many times, I believe the day you and I drop dead, the God of the Universe will look at you and me and say, "I love you very much. I will now give you what you love the most forever." If that is Him, congratulations, you are going to heaven. Now you will know what it was to be a saint. But if it's not Him — oh dear — sad for you.

That is why the greatest of all commandments is: *You shall love the Lord your God with all your heart, all your mind, all your soul, and all your strength* (see Deuteronomy 6:5 and Luke 10:27). It is not called the greatest suggestion. It's the greatest command-ment! Why? Because that is the way God loves you. He loves you with all His heart, all His mind, all His soul, and all His strength. He will not force Himself on any of us, especially not forever. So if you don't want to be with Him, He'll give you what you want.

God loves you. That is the point. When we come to know that we are loved by God, we want to respond in love. We want to be with Him who wants to be with us. If we don't want to be with Him, then He'll give us what we want. It is a choice everyone makes. Do you want to be with Him forever? Simple question — eternal answer.

While I was teaching at the boys' prep school, I was con-sidered a strong disciplinarian, but I also loved those kids and would do anything for them. I would have coffee and bagels and doughnuts in the morning and the kids would come up to my office. But in order to get to my office, they had to pass by the chapel (the tabernacle was in the center of the chapel and the doors were always wide open). The kids had to pass Jesus in the Blessed Sacrament before they walked into my office. As they would enter, I would ask them, "Did you say 'Hi' to Jesus?"

"No," they'd say.

And I would respond, "Get over there and say hi to Jesus! No doughnuts for you unless you go and acknowledge Jesus first." A lot of times they would run over and say, "Hi Jesus," and come right back to my room. "NOOO," I would say. "You go and spend time with Jesus. Tell Him that you love Him." They would walk out grumbling under their breath. Many times they were mad because they didn't want to go back.

Don't you get it? They didn't want to spend time with Jesus. I gave them the opportunity every day and I almost had to force them into being with Him. Yet I'd ask them, "Do you want to go to heaven?"

"Oh yes, Father."

"Why? I think you're a liar." I would say. "There's Jesus right there waiting for you and you can't even spend two seconds with Him every day."

See, it's the way we live our lives every day that says whether you and I love Christ or whether we're Christian atheists. If we love God, we are going to spend time with Him and we are going to obey Him. The only way you and I can prove that we love God is by being obedient. As Jesus says, If you love me, obey my commandments.

You can say all you want that you love God, but if you do not obey Him, your very actions show you do not love Him. Holiness is a process. It must be the way we are normally going, walking toward God and what God wants of us. Every once in a while, we're going to fall, and that's okay; it's our humanity. But we need to stay focused on God and want to be with Him and love Him more.

There is no reason why everybody cannot give God five minutes a day — none. There is absolutely, positively no reason. If you can't give God five minutes a day, you are a pagan who claims to be a Christian. Think about it.

When I ask men at men's conferences, "Do you pray every day?" the number one answer is, "I try." And I always want to go (whack) and hit them on the side of the head and say, "You try? Do you try to eat every day?"

"Well, no, Father."

"Do you try to go to work every day?"

"Well, no, Father."

"Do you try to read the paper every day?"

"Well, no, Father."

"Then why would you 'try' to pray? What is more important — praying or eating? If it's praying, then prove it by doing it!" If you are not praying at least five minutes a day, you are a pagan. Absolutely, positively. Read that again. If you aren't doing it, it's time you change. It is time you start saying and living, "God is what I love the most." After all, you give time to what you love. So if you have no time for God, you prove you do not love Him no matter how holy you look when you go to Communion on Sunday. It doesn't really matter if someone says, "Ooh, look how holy he looks."

If you ever want to be holy, to know God, to live His will, then the number one thing that you are going to have to do is pray. PERIOD! Nothing else matters. You cannot begin to find out God's will or even continue to read this book until you decide that you are going to spend time with God every day.

I cannot stress enough how important this is. Years ago I was preaching at a men's conference in Pennsylvania and the speaker before me said something like, "Gentlemen, I know that you are busy, but could you at least try to pray every day? You know maybe as you drive to work, just use the bumps of your steering wheel as a bead for saying the rosary and maybe you could try to say maybe a decade of the rosary every day?" I started to get madder and madder the more he spoke because he was telling the men that it is a good idea to pray, but it is so hard so just try to do it. No way!

I was the next speaker and I got up and said, "Gentlemen, you've got two choices. You pray every day, or you go to hell." (Sound familiar? Are you beginning to see a pattern?) This is what I am trying to get across to everyone. Praying is more important than breathing. It is something that we must make a regular habit in our lives. It is not an option, but a command: *Pray always* (see 1 Thessalonians 5:17).

This is the first thing that has to change in your heart and in your life. For the rest of your life, from this moment forth, you must promise Almighty God that you're not going to try to pray, but that you will pray. Every day. Period. Nothing is more important than praying. Nothing. Absolutely nothing. So live it.

One more thing. Prayer is the secret of all the saints! As we have seen, they were ordinary people; yes, ORDINARY people who, with all their hearts, strove to seek and live the will of God in their lives. When you look at some of the statues of the saints they look perfect, but saints are not statues. They had good days and bad days. They liked people and didn't like people. They had ups and downs like all of us, but they kept going. They did not look at themselves, but looked at God and sought His will. I have always defined holiness as "when God's will and our will become one." Thus, our number one goal in life must be to live God's will. We must be like the saints and look at Jesus and His grace and not us and our weaknesses.

If you look at the apostles, they were all very human men whom God chose to do His will. Each of them did that in spite of his weakness. God calls you and me in the same way — to live His will in our own personalities.

This is the type of surrender we are talking about. When we do this, no matter how dark the darkness (I say this so much because there is so much darkness in life around us), the light of Christ can never be conquered by it. We need to be people of great hope. We need to be people who, no matter how crazy life gets, no matter how bad it gets, know that God is bigger than everything.

Remember ancient Rome? Many of the Emperors tried to kill the Church; they horribly martyred us; let us be eaten by lions, but the Empire of Rome and the Emperor do not exist anymore. It's the Church of Rome that sits on top of the Roman Empire! The people who thought they had the power and who thought they were great and mighty are gone forever. Remember, the power of love always conquers the darkness. Always. So we've got to be this hope in the midst of the darkness.

This world is not our home. We are just passing through. (See 1 Peter 1:17; 2:11.) Our true home is heaven and everything we do should be to prepare us for our true home. But so often we live in such a way that it seems this is our home. Because of that, we live in constant fear of dying.

The last night that I preach at one of my parish missions, I always give the following illustration to help people get their minds around the concept of this world not being our home, and to help them not to be afraid of what is to come.

I begin by asking the kids to look at their mother's bellies. Yes, their bellies. I then continue, "You lived in there for nine months!" (This always freaks them out and they cry, "Ewwww!") I then say, "When you were in your mother's womb, you could feel her and experience her and everything came from her." The same is true for every one of you reading this book. You lived in your mother for nine months or so. You were very intimate with her. Everything she did, you did. Everything she ate or drank, you ate or drank. But you couldn't see her until you were born! Then you saw her face-to-face!

The same is true about us and God. We are in the womb of God, if you will. (This doesn't make God a woman. It's an analogy.) We can feel God, we can experience God. Everything we have comes from God, but we cannot see God until we are born to eternal life!

Anybody want to go back inside his or her mother? It's amazing nobody wants to go back. Even though you came out kicking and screaming because you liked it there, you don't want to go back. So it is with us. We like it here, but this isn't home. We can't see God because we are inside of God. He is all around us but we have to wait to be born to eternal life to see Him face-to-face.

That being said, who's the one most blessed? The one who dies at four years old or the one who dies at ninety? The one who dies at four! I know that this is an altogether different way of looking at life. But this is the Christian way of looking at life! Everybody says they are a Christian and claims to want to go to heaven, but nobody wants to die to get there. Well, there is no other way to do it.

When we start looking at life from a different perspective, then there is no fear of death because that is where I am truly supposed to be. Once I'm on the other side, there is no coming back, just like there is no going back inside your mother. You see, God gives us these images all around us to take away our fear.

We don't need to be afraid. We don't have to be afraid of the wars around us, or when the world is going to end, or who the next President of the United States will be because this world is not our home! Heaven is and God is God and He loves us, and we're going to live with Him forever.

No matter how bad it gets on the earth, our job is to bring the light of Christ to the darkness; to bring the light of the kingdom and to shine the light of salvation to everybody. We are not to curse the darkness with everybody else. When you watch the news, it seems that some Catholics are the most negative people in the world. They rant about what is wrong. They just go nuts.

When I was in the seminary, I was a complainer. I've always been a complainer. (It's just the way I am. It's not good, I know.) Anyway, one day I was complaining and my spiritual director looked at me and said, "Richards, you curse the darkness more than anybody I know. Why don't you light a light and show that you can be different?" And I did. That has been the whole point of my life. My whole priesthood, all my ministry, is purposely designed to be different. I do not want to be just like everybody else. Not even close. I want to be the light of Christ in the midst of the darkness.

It's what we all should want — to be the light of Christ. When we want that, when we surrender our life and our will to the will of the Father we become light. Remember, His will is always better than ours. His will is always life-giving. His will always brings salvation. But we need to cooperate with it.

God also gives us the power to grow in holiness. He is not just some parent who puts unrealistic expectations on us. It is by His grace that we will be all that He created us to be when we surrender to His plan.

Some people think, "I can't be holy. It is beyond me." No, it isn't. God not only calls you to holiness, He gives you all the tools to become holy. God doesn't want us to be holy and then say to us, "Good luck with that." When you and I surrender in prayer and love, that's when we experience holiness.

The vehicle of the holiness of God is the Holy Spirit. The Holy Spirit gives us His gifts and gives us His fruits to grow in holiness. But we have to use the gifts. If you have great ability to be a football player or basketball player, you have to practice every day. The gift has been given to you, but you have to work with it. You have to cooperate with it. Same with the gift of holiness.

God gives you the gift but now you have to grow in it. We have to let the Holy Spirit take control of us and then work with the Holy Spirit every day by seeking to obey the will of God in our lives.

I was having lunch with one of my students who was going through an atheist stage. (They think they are going to hit me with something I have not heard before.) He said that even if God does exist, he's mean. So I told him, "God loves you, you little pagan child, and you've got to let yourself be loved and start cooperating with that." Then he said, "But He's taking away all our fun." I said, "You don't know what fun is, son." (He was telling me about how he gets high all the time.) I told him, "Son, if you need to get high to feel good about yourself, think about how sad that is." If you need to get drunk or get high to feel good about yourself, then you are running away from something. God says, "Come to me. I'm going to help you know that you're my beloved son or my beloved daughter and you are going to feel great love. You don't need alcohol or drugs to make you feel peace inside your heart — you need love." That comes from the God of love. So instead of running to all these things that we think are going to make us happy, we go to the source of love and peace, we surrender to it and then we have happiness.

When we surrender to God's will we become an instrument of His will. It's like when we pray the St. Francis prayer, "Make me an instrument of your peace." You cannot be an instrument of peace to anybody unless peace goes through you first. You have to have peace first before you can give it to somebody else. The same is true with surrendering to His will.

Ultimately, when we surrender to His will and live it in our lives, we begin to experience heaven on earth. We can say and mean it, "Your will be done on earth as it is in heaven." So surrender and go to heaven!

STEPS TO SURRENDERING YOUR LIFE

1. Decide you want to be more in love with God and begin to commit yourself to spending time with Him. One of my top goals in life is to be a saint. Is it yours?

2. Give God permission. Your second goal needs to be to desire God's will more than your own will every day. The way you do that is that is to say, "God, your will be done in my life today." This was Jesus' prayer; it also needs to be your prayer.

3. Surrender to the Holy Spirit each day. Let Him lead you and guide you.

A Prayer to Help You on Your Way

Prayer to The Holy Spirit

Breathe in me, O Holy Spirit, that my thoughts may all be holy.
Act in me, O Holy Spirit, that my work, too, may be holy.
Draw my heart, O Holy Spirit, that I love but what is holy.
Strengthen me, O Holy Spirit, to defend all that is holy.
Guard me, then, O Holy Spirit, that I always may be holy.
Amen.

–– St. Augustine of Hippo

CHAPTER 2

Surrender and Be a Great Lover!

"If I give away everything I own, and if I hand my body over so that I may boast, but do not have love, I gain nothing." (1 Corinthians 13:3, NAB)

The only commandment Jesus Christ ever gave any of us was the commandment of love. He states, *I give you a new commandment, by your love for one another as such as my love has been for you so must your love be for each other* (see John 13:34). Then, in the next verse, He makes it very clear who His disciples are: *This is how all will know that you are my disciples, your love for one another.* Jesus tells us the way that people will know that we belong to Him is that we love one another. Boy, if only we all lived that! Christianity is a religion of love that follows a God of love, even though this is not always what the world sees coming from us. Love is the key that makes religion and our relationship with Almighty God real. St. Paul drives this point further in his famous reflection on love in 1 Corinthians 13:1–13, *If I have faith great enough to move mountains but have not love, I am nothing. If I give everything that I have to feed the poor and hand over my body to be burned, but have not love, I gain nothing.*

Jesus talks about the only commandment, but sometimes we focus only on the Ten Commandments, even fighting over if they should be in the courtrooms or out in public places. Sometimes we even say things like, "These are the Ten Commandments. We must build our lives on these Ten Commandments."

I'm here to tell you, this is only partly true! The greatest commandment, the commandment that we are called to build our lives on is the one Jesus Christ gave us. Loving one another as He commanded is the way holiness makes itself real.

Holiness expresses itself in how we deal with others! Holiness is NOT the focus on self, but the focus on others. Period.

We see this in the Old Testament in Leviticus 2:3 when God tells Moses to instruct the people, *Be holy for I the Lord your God, am holy.* Right after that, in verse 4, He states, *Revere your father and mother.* Then, in the New Testament, Jesus' words, *So be perfect, just as your heavenly Father is perfect* (see Matthew 5:48), come immediately after He tells us to love our enemies and pray for our persecutors.

In the first chapter, we talked about how we are all called to be holy. What does holiness look like? It looks like a person who is filled with love for God and love for others. The way that we prove we are living lives of holiness is that we are doing acts of love. We need to be love in a world that doesn't know love!

Love is always going to be in the will of God. If we do anything that doesn't contain love, we can be sure it's not the will of God because God is love. As a priest, I can say Mass every day. I can pray many rosaries every day. But if I'm not doing those things in love, they are not the will of God.

Remember, God wants you and me to be His presence in the world. In order to do that, we need to remember what a Christian is. A Christian is not just a person who lives a moral life. Some good atheists live moral lives. Some Jewish people live moral lives. Some Muslims live moral lives. Being a moral person does not make one a Christian. A Christian, by definition, is one who no longer lives his life, but Jesus Christ lives inside and through him.

Being a Christian is going to cost you your life. If it doesn't cost you your life, you're not a Christian yet. You may have been baptized. You may be going through the motions. You may be doing all the right things, but, as St. Paul says in one of my favorite verses, *I have been crucified with Christ. So the life I live now is no longer my own, Jesus Christ lives inside of me. I still live my human life, yes, but it is of faith in the Son of God who loved me and gave His life for me* (see Galatians 2:19). So that's what we really must do — die to ourselves so that Christ might live in us.

Our job as Christians is to get out of the way and let Christ love through us. That's the hardest part of being Christian. Somehow we always get in the way of Christ. The biggest temptation is to let our own ego get in front of everything else. I know I can do that way too often. It doesn't matter if thousands of people listen to me or read my books. If my work isn't done in love, it is for nothing. What needs to happen is that we do God's work with love. As we talked about in the first chapter, this must be done in reality. Love, holiness and humility need to be real, not a nice thought or a good intention.

Some people think being a loving person means we are always nice. If you think that, read the Scriptures. Christ was not always nice. Remember, He once called a woman a *dog* (see Mark 7:27). In His humanity, Jesus had bad days like everybody else. It wasn't as if every time somebody came into His presence they just felt the love oozing. Some people, when they were with Him, wanted to kill Him. A lot of people would not welcome Christ in our churches today because He would make then uncomfortable, just like He made the people of His time feel uncomfortable. But He did everything in love.

Sometimes love is hard. Look at how you treat your children, if you have them. I bet that sometimes you punish them. Is it because you hate them? No, it's because you love them. But while you are punishing them, they might think that's not a great thing, even though you are doing it because you love them.

When I have a Question and Answer session (Q & A sessions usually get me into more problems than anything else), people will ask, "Father, do you think God punishes us?" They always expect me to say, "No, God doesn't punish us because God is love." If they expect that answer from me, they don't know me. I always answer, "Well let's see what God's Word says about your question" and then I read Hebrews 12:5–10:

> You have also forgotten the exhortation addressed to you as sons: "My sons, do not disdain the discipline of the Lord nor lose heart when He reproves you; for whom the Lord loves, He disciplines; he scourges every son he receives." Endure your trials as the discipline of God, who deals with you as sons. For what son is there whom his father does not discipline?
>
> If you do not know the discipline of sons, you are not sons but bastards. If we respected our earthly fathers who corrected us, should we not all the more submit to the Father of Spirits, and live? They disciplined us as seemed right to them, to prepare us for the short span of mortal life; but God does so for our true benefit, that we may share His holiness.

This surprises some people because they think discipline cannot be part of a God of love, but it is according to His Word. (Sorry, but that's what it says.) When we talk about this God of love, it means that He does everything in His power to save us, to love us, to make us better. It's just like when we were growing up with our parents; sometime they had to discipline us. Sometimes our parents had to be hard on us. The same is true with the God of Love. But you always have to understand that whatever happens to you, it's because He loves you, not because He is out to get you.

Now when I talk about the discipline of God, I am not talking about God saying something like, "Well, you did something bad, so now you'll get cancer." That would be a God of evil, not a God of love. That would be a God of terrible vengeance. No, no. God's discipline would be as if you catch your son or daughter playing with matches. Instead of being politically correct and saying, "Okay, you are going to go to time out," most people would say, "Come here! (Whack!)" And slap their child's fingers so they never play with matches again. Did you slap their hands because you hate them? No. You did it because you love them. It's the same with God.

We have to be careful when we talk about living a life of love and service. Love means that you do what's best for people to get them into heaven. That's what love is. Jesus did what He did for the love of us — to get us to heaven. That primarily means He had to die for us. When you are going to love people, when you are going to die for them and put them in front of yourself, then, *Your attitude must be that of Christ . . . He accepted even death, death on a cross!* (see Philippians 2:8).

Take the example of Padre Pio. I'd be petrified to go to him for confession. If you've ever read anything by him or any of the stories about him, you know why. He might throw you out of the confessional! (Could you imagine if I did that just once? Everybody would say, "Father Larry is so mean. He threw me out of confession." But Padre Pio did it a lot, He would sometimes tell a person, "No, you are not ready. Get out!" Whoa! Did he hate these people? No way. He loved them and he wanted them to go to heaven, so he had to do things to shock them to get them to see the reality of what they were doing.

Sometimes love is like that, but love always entails giving your life for others. Jesus commands us in John 13:34, *Love one another as I have loved you.* Then He says, *There is no other greater love than this than to lay down your life for your friends* (see John 15:13). Finally, He gives us an example by giving His own life. What this means is if we are going to do the will of

God, every day is going to be a day of self-sacrifice. Again, to make this real and practical I tell people that they should examine their consciences every night before they go to bed and ask, "Did I do at least one act of unselfishness today? Did I give my life away at least once today?" If the answer is no, then they squandered the whole day on themselves, only did what they wanted, only took care of themselves. What a waste of a day!

Every day we must give our lives away. Usually it will happen in ways we don't want to do. Take the day I was walking out of my office to see somebody in the hospital. I just got the call and I had to get over there. As I was walking out the door, someone grabbed me, literally grabbed me, and asked, "Father, can you hear my confession?" "Right now?" I asked, and she responded, "Yes, please." I was thinking, No way. I've got to get over to the hospital. You are interrupting my plan for the day! But I said "Okay," and I heard her confession. It was a great confession! But I didn't want to do it. It went against the way I felt. Was it an act of love? Yes! It didn't feel like it though. My original plan was a good plan. It was an act of love, too. I was going to the hospital to anoint somebody. But God wanted me to give another act of love to somebody else first. It wasn't part of my plan, but it was a part of His plan.

Have you ever had something like this happen to you?

There are days I don't want to be generous or loving or whatever God happens to call me to do. So what? I must do it anyway. That is love.

When we are going to do the will of God, we are going to have to do it whether we feel like it or not. That's why one of my favorite Scripture stories is the parable of the two sons. I'm sure you know the one. It is found in Matthew 21:28–32. The father tells the one son to go into the vineyard and do this and that. The first son says, *Absolutely not. I'm not doing it.* Then the father tells his other son, who says, *Okay, yeah, sure I'll do it.*

Then the first son, who said he wasn't going to do it, did it anyway. The second son, who said he was going to do it, didn't do it at all. Jesus asks, *Which of the two did what the father wanted?* We all know the answer.

As the old saying goes, "The road to hell is paved by good intentions." We need to do whatever God asks. It's as simple as that. Are we going to do God's will even if we don't want to? That's the real question isn't it?

When Jesus Christ was confronted with the will of His Father in the Garden of Gethsemane, did He smile and say, "Oh, thank you, Father. I just want to suffer and die today for you" with a big smile on His face? No, He pleaded with His Father and begged, *Father, if it is your will, take this cup away from me; yet not my will but yours be done.* He tells His Father that He will do whatever He wants, even if it kills Him — and it does!

I know this is so different from what we hear from so many preachers today. Too many preachers preach that God just wants to bless us and have us be to be happy on earth. But God loved His Son more than anyone or anything, and if He asked His Son to deny Himself for others, how much more will He ask of us? Thus, being a Christian or a disciple of Jesus is not about getting what we want. It is about doing what God wants! It is not about what we feel. It's about doing what He wants! Being a Christian has nothing to do with feelings. It has everything to do with action.

Do it anyway, even if you don't feel like it. That is how you carry out the reality of true love in your life. There is a great example of this in the life of St. Thérèse, the Little Flower. She couldn't stand someone in her community. (Can you imagine a saint who didn't like someone?) Every time this other sister walked in, St. Thérèse would sit there and think, "Ugh!" But then she would go out of her way, she would go against her feelings, to treat this sister with great love and compassion and to do nice things for her. One day the sister came up to her and asked, "Why do you always smile at me? Why are you always so kind, even when I treat you badly?" Read her autobiography, *The Story of a Soul*; it's all in there.

Some people would say that is hypocrisy. Other people would say that St. Thérèse was laying down her life for someone else. She died to her feelings to be an instrument of God to somebody else.

The reality is there are some people that seem impossible to love. Down by the railroad tracks near Erie, Pennsylvania, a man raped and killed a two-year-old girl. When I heard about it, I was full of anger and outrage. What a horrible act! Yet God loves that person with all His heart and died for him. Then God looks at you and me and says, *Oh, see how you have judged him, but I commanded you to judge not!* (see Matthew 7:1). *Now I want you to love him.* Impossible, you say! I know. That's why you've got to get out of the way and let Jesus do it through you.

So often we let ourselves be limited by our strength or weakness, but we must continue the will of God in the world today by letting Christ live inside of us. When we find someone impossible to love, we must get out of the way and say, "I can't love them Lord, but you can. I give you permission. You love them through me, Lord. Make me an instrument of love today, Lord. Even if I don't want to do it. Make me love the unlovable, even if I don't want to do it."

When I taught at Cathedral Prep, I was a very easy teacher, but I was also a hard disciplinarian. Every Friday I'd give the boys a test. Every Thursday I would give them the answers to every single question. I would say something like this, "Listen, tomorrow is the test. This is the first question: 'Who was Abraham?' Gentlemen, the answer is 'the Father of the faith.' The second question is 'Who was Sara?' The answer, gentleman, is 'the wife of Abraham.'" I did this every week for all eight years that I taught there, and every year I would fail an average of eight boys!

I gave them all the questions and all the answers to every single test and yet they just didn't care. God does the same thing. He gives us the questions and answers to the final exam in Matthew 25:31–46. It is here that He tells us what the last judgment will be like:

> When the Son of Man comes in His glory, and all the angels with Him, He will sit upon his glorious throne, and all the nations will be assembled before Him. And He will separate them one from another, as a shepherd separates the sheep from the goats. He will place the sheep on His right and the goats on His left. Then the king will say to those on His right, "Come, you who are blessed by my Father. Inherit the kingdom prepared for you from the foundation of the world.
>
> "For I was hungry and you gave me food, I was thirsty and you gave me drink, a stranger and you welcomed me, naked and you clothed me, ill and you cared for me, in prison and you visited me."
>
> Then the righteous will answer Him and say, "Lord, when did we see you hungry and feed you, or thirsty and give you drink? When did we see you a stranger and welcome you, or naked and clothe you? When did we see you ill or in prison, and visit you?" And the king will say to them in reply, "Amen, I say to you, whatever you did for one of these least brothers of mine, you did for me." Then He will say to those on his left, "Depart from me, you accursed, into the eternal fire prepared for the devil and his angels. For I was hungry and you gave me no food, I was thirsty and you gave me no drink, a stranger and you gave me no welcome, naked and you gave me no clothing, ill and in prison, and you did not care for me." Then they will

answer and say, "Lord, when did we see you hungry or thirsty or a stranger or naked or ill or in prison, and not minister to your needs?" He will answer them, "Amen, I say to you, what you did not do for one of these least ones, you did not do for me." And these will go off to eternal punishment, but the righteous to eternal life.

Isn't it amazing that the just do not know they are being saved?

Pastor Craig Groeschel tells a story that happened to him when he was a little boy. When he was a kid, he went to Vacation Bible School. There the teacher separated everyone and asked, "Okay, kids, if you were to die today, how many of you know that you are going right to heaven?" Craig and a bunch of other kids didn't raise their hands. So the teacher went on, "Because if you don't know you're going to heaven, you're going to hell!" And this kid who became a Christian pastor ran out of the church and never stopped running until he got to his home. After that, his prayer every night was, "Lord, please don't send me to hell. Lord, please don't send me to hell." Again and again. "Please don't send me to hell. Please don't send me to hell."

Can you imagine that? People think I'm hard. I would never in a billion years tell kids, "If you don't know you're going to heaven, you're going to hell." Talk about abuse! Sorry if this bursts your bubble, but according to Matthew 25, you can't be positive you are going to heaven because the saved don't know they are being saved!

At the end of our lives, we will be judged by how we have loved or failed to love. That is the ultimate test: how we dealt with the least of our brothers and sisters, the people we can't stand. One of our modern day soon-to-be saints, Dorothy Day, said it this way, "I really only love God as much I love the person I love the least." This is just another way of saying what Jesus tells us. We love God as much as the person we love the least. So think about the person you just can't stand, the person that hurt you, the person who rubs you the wrong way. Do you have a clear image of them? Are you feeling all those negative feelings for them? That's how much you love God. (Do you hate me yet?)

Love is hard. It is not like we hear in all our modern love songs. Love begins when you are willing to lay down your life for the person on the bottom of your list, the one you can't stand. That is love.

I like to say that we begin to know what it is to love like God when we start to hope that the person we can't stand the most gets to sit right next to us in heaven for all eternity! What a hard thought. This is why we need God's Amazing Grace. It takes the God of the Universe to love others in us and through us. That person on the bottom of your list is someone whom God loved and gave His life for. He tells us, "I want you to be my instrument of love to that person." And we respond, "Oh no, I don't think so." But God encourages us, "That's what I want you to do. I want you to be love in a world that does not know love."

St. John of the Cross says, "Where there is no love, put love. And then you will find love."[2] Read that again and let the words sink in. God can change our hearts if we surrender them to Him!

I like to tell the story of Justin Fatica, who was one of my students at Prep. I just couldn't stand him. The Lord commands us to pray for our enemies and I saw him as an enemy. He was disrespectful and rude. (Did I say I could not stand this kid?) So I put him on my prayer list. I started praying for him every day, asking the Lord to bring Justin into a relationship with Him and to change my heart toward Justin.

As I was praying for him, I still wanted to kill him, but I knew that following Jesus is not about how you feel. Jesus commanded me to pray for him and I knew Jesus loved him, so

I tried. One day the Lord told me to ask Justin to a retreat I was starting. I told the Lord, "No," but He would not take that answer, so I did what I was told and asked Justin to the retreat. Well, he came to the retreat and had a great conversion. Now he goes throughout the world as a lay evangelist bringing many young people to Jesus. By going against the way I was feeling and by being obedient to God's will, God was able to use a very imperfect instrument to make Justin into a great person of the Gospel. I wish I could say I've done that with a lot of people. There still are people I need to allow the Lord to change my heart toward.

You want to start loving the people you can't stand? (Say yes.) Here is a practical way to help you. Make a list of the people who have hurt you, or you hate, or just don't like for whatever reason. Then start praying for each of them by name every day. Ask God to bless them and beg Him to change your heart toward them. Now for some of you this is just about going to kill you. Good! It is about time you start loving the way God has commanded instead of just the way you want!

Love always leads to service. Years ago, I was in Rome and had the chance to say Mass with a priest friend of mine for Bl. Mother Teresa's Missionaries of Charity. While I was at the convent having breakfast after Mass, I was struck by a framed saying of Mother's that hung on the wall:

> The fruit of silence is PRAYER
> The fruit of prayer is FAITH
> The fruit of faith is LOVE
> The fruit of love is SERVICE
> The fruit of service is PEACE

I have this framed and on the wall in my bathroom to remind me every day that prayer leads to faith, love, and service. When we are people of love, our fruit manifests itself when we become people of service. Whenever you are struggling to find God's will in your life, know it always involves your becoming more loving and living a life of service. Always!

People often ask me, "Father, I don't know if I should marry this person or if I should be a priest." Or, "Should I do this or should I do that?" I always answer, "Do whatever is going to make you more loving and a better servant. Will this make you more loving? Will it help you to give away your life and service?" Vocation is not about doing what you want; it is about doing what God wants, and this always has to do with service.

Think about Mary. When Mary became the Mother of God, when she said yes to the will of the Father, she carried the God of the Universe inside her. Now if anybody in all eternity got to say, "You know, I must take care of myself first. I have God as a little baby inside of me," it was her! But she didn't do that. What was the first thing she did? She served! She made haste and went to take care of Elizabeth, her cousin (see Luke 1:39–56). She had to leave her home and travel a great distance to take care of somebody else first. Before she took care of herself! Isn't that amazing? God blessed Mary abundantly when she said yes to Him. Then He sent her to serve Elizabeth. Mary did it, gladly. She put Elizabeth before herself.

How different is that from most of the "self-help" books of today! They constantly teach that we must take care of ourselves before we can take care of anybody else. People of God, that's absolute garbage and not the gospel of Jesus Christ! The gospel teaches us that if you give away your life, then you are going to find life — the total opposite of what the world teaches. The world buys into the "Burger King theology" — "Have it your way" — take care of yourself first. Ugh!

So who took care of Mary? God. And Joseph. When you put yourself last, God puts you first. The world tells you to put yourself first, take care of number one, no one else is going to do it, but that's not what God says. When you are discerning God's will, it is always going to be about taking care of somebody else or even before yourself, always.

It amazes me that the biggest part of every bookstore is the self-help section. Why is it so big? After people read the first self-help book, what do they do? They get another one. I have a good friend who goes through many self-help books. He is always saying, "Hey Father, you've got to read this one." He is always looking for the latest and greatest guru. But none of these has brought him peace. He is always worried. I gotta take care of my family. I gotta make sure I have . . . I gotta make sure they like me . . . I gotta make sure I make enough money. Gotta make sure I am healthy. I gotta make sure I have enough for retirement. I gotta make sure that I am organized. Okay I get it, but get this — none of those things will bring him or anyone else peace and everlasting life!

That is not the way Christ or His Mother lived their lives. They gave everything away. It's not the way the saints lived their lives. They gave everything away. They put other people in front of them. When you are trying to discern your vocation, trying to discern God's will, it will always involve love and service.

What we have to do is take care of all the people who are least on our list, but we also have to watch out for "false humility." You know what I mean — the person who says, "Oh, I'm not worthy. Oh, I'm such a lowly worm," as they play this "holy" game. There's a lot of "false humility" that makes itself into the Church. People think they are holy if they have it. I think the exact opposite.

When the Mother of God was asked to be the Mother of God, she did not say, "Oh, I'm not worthy. You better pick someone else to be God's Mother." She just said, *Fiat, let it be done to me as you say* (see Luke 1:38) or, to put it in modern language,

"If this is what you want, then this is what I want. I want what you want." No false humility in Mary.

Humility is truth. It is truth about who we are. It is knowing ourselves intimately, but it is not a focus on self. I believe that "false humility" is always focused on self, and "true humility" is always focused on God and others. Now, we are not talking about hating yourself. We are talking about living your life for others, and you can't do that unless you love yourself.

As I said before, Jesus got His power and strength in His humanity, from hearing the Father say, *You are My Beloved Son* (see Mark 1:11). When Jesus came to know He was beloved, then He could gladly give His life away for others. This again is where prayer comes in. You must know that you are loved. You must spend time in His arms every day! We will focus on this more in Chapter 4.

Many people live fearing that if they give away their lives, they will end up with nothing. Do you really think that you can out give God? I will never forget the day I took my vow of celibacy. It was on October 15, 1988. I went to my spiritual director, Father Peterson, a week before and said, "I'm not so sure I can take this vow of celibacy." He looked at me, and with one of his famous one-liners, said, "Richards, your problem isn't with celibacy; it's with humility." (Thank you, Father.) I sat there and finally said, "Okay, Pete, but I'm not so sure about this." Then he said, "Just shut up and go and pray" (which he told me all the time). So before I went to bed that night, I just prayed, "Lord, if this is what you want then I will do it, but I want kids. I want kids." It was my big line to the Lord — "I want kids." I then fell asleep and woke up in the middle of the night because a relic I had of St. Teresa of Ávila flew off the mantle and hit the bottom of my bed. I'm telling you the honest to goodness truth. It was October 15, the Feast Day of St. Teresa, and so she really got my attention and so I started praying again about taking my vow of celibacy. I just kept saying, "Lord, I want kids. I'm not sure I can do this, but Lord I trust in you." I went to sleep and I realized that it was God's will for me not to have children. He was going to do the world a huge favor by not having "little Larrys" running around everywhere. God said to me, "Richards, you are the last of them."

So later that day I took my vow of celibacy, and when Bishop Michael Murphy said: Therefore, I ask you: In the presence of God and the Church, are you resolved, as a sign of your interior dedication to Christ, to remain celibate for the sake of the kingdom and in lifelong service to God and mankind? And I responded: "I am," and I put on the ring I always wear on my left hand (which I can no longer get off because I got too fat), which states all around it; "Love one another as I have loved you." The quote, of course, is what Jesus commanded us to do in John 13:34. It reminds me very clearly that I must love the way God has commanded me. This is what I must do. I don't always live it well, but this is my ideal.

I will never forget right after I took my vow of celibacy, I put the ring on and sat there. I was thinking, "You got it all now, Lord." I knew I was never going to give it up. With God's grace, I am more than 50 years old and still a virgin by choice. (I know some of you are thinking, "Father, who'd sleep with you?" but I've had my chances, thank you very much.) I knew when I made my vow that I would never, ever experience what most people experience. There was a little bit of sadness inside because I knew that I would never know sexual intimacy, and I would not have my own children. I knew it would be a struggle in some ways, but I took it on because this is what Jesus asked of me, so by His grace I would do it for love of Him and His people.

I thought I gave something up for God and that I was doing God a big favor. My spiritual director likes to look at me and say, "You know, Larry, you didn't do God a favor by becoming a priest," because there are days I think I did. I think that I could be doing others, but then God reminds me, "This is what I created you for." So whenever I think that I'm doing God a favor, my spiritual director reminds me I am not!

Anyway, I put on celibacy even though I knew I'd never have kids and I'd never be intimate with another person that way. Right after I took my vow, I attended a big youth group called TOUCH (Teen Outreach United Christian Hands). I had the biggest youth group in the diocese with 160 kids. (This was in 1988, before any of the scandals.) Afterwards the kids came up to me and said, "Father, we got you some presents." This was the first time they called me Father and I said, "What did you get me, you little pagans?" One of the gifts they got me was a plaque with the Peace Prayer of St. Francis, which I have in my room. They knew how much love I have for St. Francis, so I said, "Thank you!" Then they said, "We got you something else," and they handed me a little box. I opened the box, and in it there was a medal of St. Christopher. I said, "Oh, St. Christopher" (they knew the way I drove), and then they said to me, "Oh shut up and read the back." (Those little pagans! The way they talked to me!) Now, you can hardly see it, but on the back, it reads:

10-15-88.
Congratulations.
We love you.
Larry's kids.

I had never called them "Larry's kids." My last words to God the night before were, "I want kids," and the next day He gave me 160 of them! What a God! I thought I was doing God a favor. I thought I was giving up children, and God said, "Are you a fool? You really think you can be more generous than I?"

The answer is no. Absolutely not. When you and I are generous with God, He is always much more generous with us.

When it comes to being generous, every Christian, by definition, must take care of the poor in some way or another. You must. It can't be an afterthought. On average, 24,000 children die every day in the world because of poverty-related illnesses. What are you going to do when you stand before God and He asks, "How come in your lifetime 24,000 children died everyday because of starvation? I gave you abundantly so that you can take care of them. But you went and took care of yourself first." What are you going to do? Look at Him and say, "Well they weren't my kids"? He'll say, "No . . . they were Mine. I gave you abundantly so you could share with them so they could live. You chose to spend it all on yourself."

People of God, to be saved you must take care of the poor! You have to do it consistently. That's why I encourage you to adopt a kid in a Third World country. It'll cost you 30 bucks a month. $30! Yeah, a dollar a day, you poor person. I don't want to hear about how expensive it is. Everybody can afford it. Stop going to McDonald's every day for your $1 coffee. Let's see. Coffee for yourself every morning or giving it up so someone can live another day? Hmmm, such a choice. To do the will of God you must take care of the poor. It's that simple.

The second thing we need to do is take care of our families. So often people look really holy in church, but they are terrible with their families. (That's including priests, too.) As Bl. Mother Teresa said, love your families first. So we must serve them first and then your parish, your community or the world. But you have to take care of family first. For those of you who are married, one way you experience Christ, is through your spouse. Your spouse is your sacrament of Christ to you, by definition. Now you might look at me and say, "Father, my spouse is a pagan." Then I'd ask why did you marry him or her? I used to tell my boys at Prep, "Gentlemen, don't you ever marry anybody unless they love Jesus more than they love you." The boys would say, "Father that is a high standard," and I'd reply, "I'd have a high standard to be married to somebody for the rest of my life!" You become the sacrament of Christ to your spouse and so you have to love them first.

The same with your kids. Your kids, every one of your kids, are not made in your image and likeness. They are made in God's image and likeness. Your job is to love them first. Try to make it practical. What do you do every day to love your husband or wife or for your sons or daughters? You might say, "Well, I go and work for them." Nice. When you come home, do you listen to them? Do you talk to them? Do you tuck your kids in? Do you ask your wife or husband, how are you today? A family must be a place of great intimacy, a place where you go beyond what people see on the exterior and see what is going on in the inside of a person.

Let me explain what I mean. I have an anger problem. I went to counseling for anger. I have even attended anger management classes. Anger is usually not the core problem, but a symptom of something much deeper. The problem is usually either fear or hurt, and anger is the way we protect ourselves and keep people at a distance.

It seems that everyone wants something from me, so I have sometimes used anger to keep them at a distance. It's just reality. It's the way I stay celibate. It's the thing that has worked best, and worst, for me throughout the years. I am not proud of it, but it is just part of my own sinfulness. Anyway, a couple of years ago, I had just about had it with always giving, giving, giving. I had been on the road a lot speaking, as well as doing everything in the parish. I just couldn't take it anymore. And it was Christmas, always a stress-filled time for me, anyway. I remember going home and I was a mess, almost ready to lose it. Not lose it in anger, but just lose it emotionally. I just couldn't give anymore. So I went to Pittsburgh to my mother's house on Christmas Day, walked in and dropped off the presents upstairs and said, "Merry Christmas," and went downstairs alone and just closed the door. A few minutes later my mother, who is a little German lady, didn't let me be alone. She walked into the room, came and sat in front of me and said, "So what's the matter?"

She was the first person in months to ask if I was okay. She went beyond my anger and negative attitude and went deeper to find out how I was on the inside. She saw me. That's what I mean by intimacy.

Is your family a place of intimacy? If you have a husband who has a problem with anger and you just say, "You better stop getting angry!" what do they do? Get angrier. Because you're not dealing with the problem, you are dealing with the symptom. If you look at him and ask, "Why are you hurting? What are you afraid of?" you will help stop the anger faster than any other thing.

People expect to have intimacy at home but they usually don't have it there. So I'll ask again, is your home a place of intimacy. Is your family a place of affirmation?

Years ago, I was giving a men's talk in Kansas City (those poor men, they had to listen to me all day!). There was a kid in the back of the Church with black hair in a Mohawk. He had on a long pea coat and was wearing big black boots.

The whole time I was talking, I could tell I wasn't reaching this kid. The more I was speaking the more he seemed to be getting bored. At the end of the day, I was literally running out, saying goodbye, because I had to leave to give a parish mission and this kid comes running up toward me. I thought, "Oh he's going to kill me." But he said, "Father, Father," and he handed me this little piece of paper. At first I thought it was a hate letter, saying he was mad at something I said. But when I got to the car I looked at the folded piece of paper and written on the outside was, "*Pax Omni*," which means: "Peace everywhere." As I opened up the paper this is what it said: "Maybe one person in a thousand years dies from too much praise. Yet every minute, a kid dies inside from lack of it." (By the way, I have carried this paper with me in my Bible since that time to remind me that people are not always as they seem.)

It hit me right between the eyes, and I thought, "Whoa, do we affirm the people in our families?" It's God's will that we do. Do we build them up or do we tear them down? Even if you have to discipline your kids and sometimes have to be hard on them, do you affirm them every day?

I will never forget one time when my dad was really hard on me. He had to be. He made me do something. I don't remember what it was, but I remember him grabbing and hugging me and saying, "Larry, I love you very much. That's why I'm doing this."

Is that what we do when we discipline our kids? Do we tell them that we love them and that's why we do it? Are we affirming one another in our family? Do we build one another up? This is what God is calling us to.

When it comes to being a generous person toward the church, the parish you belong to, your community, as a whole, are we people who are givers or are we takers? I've said a million times — there is no such thing as a "taker" in Christianity. There are only givers. Every gift you and I have been given, we are given it for the service of others.

As a priest I have been given gifts. Not one of those gifts was given to me for me, now were they? I cannot look in the mirror and say, "Hey, Larry, are you sorry for your sins?" and look back in the mirror and say, "Oh yes, Father, I'm sorry for my sins," and then tell myself, "Now I absolve you of your sins." If I could forgive myself my sins that would be a great trick, now wouldn't it? I do not have the power to forgive myself my sins. I can't baptize myself. I can't anoint myself. Not one gift given to me as a priest was given to me for me. Every gift I have been given was given to me for thee.

It is the same with you. Every gift you and I have been given, God gave you for the building up of the body, the church. God created us in this beauty of His body to build up the body. If you use your gifts just to make money, if you use them just to take care of your family, if you use them just to take care of yourself or to build a name for yourself, you are wasting the gifts that God gave you. You are hurting the body of Christ. He gave you your gifts so you can build up the Church, the body of Christ.

That is part of your vocation, part of your ministry in the Church, and every one of us has our own part to play. You might think you cannot do much, but you can pray. Every single person, when it comes to ministry, can be an intercessor. The most powerful moment in our lives is when we can pray for others. What is Jesus doing right now? He is interceding for us.

Some people look at the Carmelite nuns, who spend their lives in a cloistered monastery in prayer and say, "Oh, what a wasted life!" Are you kidding me? Their whole life is given for us. They are praying for us. I often say the reason I am effective in doing what I do is because I have had Carmelite nuns pray for me by name every day since I was a young seminarian. For more than 30 years these nuns have prayed for me every day.

Not only have these holy nuns prayed for me throughout the years, but when I am out preaching God's Word and doing His will. My parish members also intercede for me every day. There is a little stand in my parish chapel in the Perpetual Adoration chapel on a table in front of the Blessed Sacrament which has information about where I am ministering and asks them to pray for me and the people I am speaking to. There are also people all over the world who pray for me on a daily basis — maybe you can become one of those people. It is the intercession of others and the Grace of Almighty God that gives me the power and strength to do what I do.

Sometimes people focus way too much on their own weaknesses or lack of talents and have a little "pity party." Think about this, when was Christ most powerful? When He was on the cross! When He seemed most un-powerful, most weak, most vulnerable is when He saved the world! When you and I are most weak is when God can use us for His glory. He says to us the same thing He said to St. Paul: *My grace is sufficient for you, for my power is made perfect in weakness* (see 2 Corinthians 12:9). As long as you are alive, God has a perfect plan in His will for you today or you would not be alive. Trust in Him and His power, not on you and your weakness!

Doing God's Will always involves love and service. If you are in a nursing home or you can't get out, you can really love people by praying for them and by interceding for them. By doing that, you are showing them you love them. Every time you do that, you become an instrument of Grace.

Let me give you an example. When the sun is out, take a magnifying glass. Hold the magnifying glass out in front of you over the top of a piece of paper. The magnifying glass will focus the rays of the sun through the magnifying glass and set that piece of paper on fire. When you and I intercede and pray for people, we become spiritual magnifying glasses. The grace of God will be all around us. There's no place where you can't find the grace of God. When you and I pray for people, we place ourselves over them. God's grace is magnified and directed through us and sets them on fire by the power of the Holy Spirit. So be an intercessor and pray for others. It's the greatest thing you can ever do — to really pray for them. Another thing is to fast for them. When you fast, it's kind of like taking the dirt that is on the magnifying glass and cleaning it off. It focuses the prayer even more.

If you have children who do not know Christ, are you praying for them? You might tell me that you have been praying for them for 20 years, but I will tell you that Monica prayed for Augustine for 30 years and he is a great saint. So is she, by the way. He came to Christ because of his mother's prayers. The same can be true for you!

When you do not think you have much to give, you have lots to give. You can pray and intercede for the people of the world. To remind you of this, a good thing to do is to keep a crucifix in your room, and when you think you are weak and you think you are not making any difference, look at that crucifix, that sign of love and service. The crucifix is a sign that Jesus' greatest moment in the world was when people thought He was defeated. The crucifix points to the greatest moment in history.

In our own lives, when we feel weak, we can look at the crucifix and see Jesus. He transformed the world. He said to us that through His suffering and pain, He wants to transform it with us. This is what St. Paul meant when he said *we unite in our suffering and with the sufferings of Christ* (see Colossians 1:24).

A wonderful practice to develop is to learn to "offer things up." This is a way that we can unite our sufferings with Christ for others. This used to be a much-taught practice in the Church, but it has not been taught as much lately. I think this is very sad because it keeps us from great power and consolation.

When I was learning to be a chaplain in a hospital, there was a woman in her early 20s who had been in a car accident with her brother who was drinking and driving. When I walked into her room, she was in terrible pain. She was also filled with anger at her brother. I asked her if she wanted to get over this, and she said she did. I then told her to forgive her brother and offer up her pain for his good. She did not like that at all. She screamed at me, and threw me out of the room. All because I told her to forgive her bother and to offer up her pain.

A couple of days later the nurses called me and told me she wanted to see me. I walked into the room and saw this girl smiling from ear to ear. I asked, "What's up?" She had told me she didn't like me the other day (join the crowd, then, huh?). She said, "I was so angry with what you said to me. But then I thought I'm suffering anyway, why not try it? So I forgave my brother. I called him. I forgave him. Then I offered up the pain for him. You know what happened? My pain went away."

Ding, ding, ding, ding! You see what happens when we offer things up? Sometimes you can offer it up for the person who hurt you and the suffering might get worse. But it's bringing salvation. You become another Christ in the world. Instead of going through life talking about what is wrong and how bad things are, offer up the pain. Transform the world. Bring others to salvation. Be Christ on earth. This is the will of God — that you and I become Christ's love on earth. That's your vocation and its time we live it.

STEPS TO SURRENDERING YOUR LIFE

1. Ask God how He wants you to love and serve. Tell Him you will do anything that He asks.
2. Write down the names of people you don't like and start asking God to change your heart toward them so that you can love them the way He does.
3. Become an intercessor and start praying for people.
4. Learn to "offer things up." Unite your suffering with the suffering of Christ and start transforming the world.

A PRAYER TO HELP YOU ON YOUR WAY

Prayer for the Miracle of God's Love[3]

Our Father, here I am, at your disposal, your child,
use me to continue your loving the world,
by giving Jesus to me and through me,
to each other and to the world.
Let us pray for each other, that we allow Jesus
to love in us, and through us,
with the love with which His Father loves Him.
Amen.

— BL. MOTHER TERESA OF CALCUTTA

CHAPTER 3

Surrender and Be Free!

"Everyone who commits sin is a slave of sin. A slave does not remain in a household forever, but a son always remains. So if a son frees you, then you will truly be free." (John 8:34–36, NAB)

When it comes to discerning God's will, a person must be free to discern. We can't be a slave to anything — to our passions, to the world, to the devil, to anything. We need to be free. But how do we become slaves?

Jesus tells us that anyone who sins is a slave. I know that this is the exact opposite of what the world says. The world says when you are doing God's will, all He does is put rules on you. And when you live by these rules, you're a slave to God.

In one way that is true. I even preach a lot that you've got to be a slave to Jesus Christ. Paul introduced himself that way, *I, Paul, a slave of Jesus Christ* (see Titus 1:1). When we read the lives of the saints, a lot of them made themselves slaves of Jesus and of the Blessed Mother. But this is a slavery of love! It's a free slavery. It's a slavery that we choose and we desire because we're in love with Almighty God, who loves us so much.

Some of the years when I was chaplain at the boys' school, I was also the chaplain at Penn State Behrend College, which had, at the time, about 3,000 students. Since I was a night person, and still am in a lot of ways, I would go out to Behrend College at 1:00 a.m. on Friday or Saturday night. All the kids were up and I could meet them where they were. When I got there, the word would spread, "Father Larry's here! Father Larry's here!" and everybody would come and start asking me questions about all kinds of things. I love when people are questioning things for it shows that they are searching for Truth, and God Who is Ultimate Truth can answer every question they have.

I don't know what the rules are exactly today, but they used to have a rule at the state university where I served as a chaplain that you're not allowed to have someone of the opposite sex in your room for more than three days. After three days, you've got to change rooms. (Not a good practice for morality.)

Here are all these young adults with their first taste of what they think is "freedom." They can do anything they want. No parents there to watch and impose rules. The kids are away from their families, away from everything else and they think, "I can do anything I want!" I can get drunk every night. I can get high every night. I can have sex every night. I can do anything I want!" FREEDOM, right? And a lot of these kids go ahead and do anything they want.

One night I was walking through the campus and literally passed more than 100 kids. (Yes, I counted them.) Not one of them had a smile on their face. Can you imagine? You mean if you can get drunk every night, if you can get high, if you can have sex with anyone you want, you are not going to be happy? Yeah, that is what I'm saying. Isn't it amazing that when you and I start doing things that are against the will of God, all it does is make us emptier?

Every one of us has a hole inside of our heart and we are constantly trying to fill it up. We think if we try to fill it up with this or fill it up with that (you fill in the blanks) we're going to be happy. But everything in this world is temporary.

When I do a high school retreat, I start out my confession talk by saying, "Kids, you know, we're always trying to fill up our emptiness. It is like we've all got this hole inside of us and it was given to us when we inherited original sin. Original sin — when Adam and Eve were with God they were happy and had everything they wanted and could do anything. They were so happy with God and yet when they sinned — BANG! A hole got knocked into their soul and throughout all of eternity we've always been trying to fill up the emptiness."

Bl. Mother Teresa used to say people in India were so hungry that they would actually go around, pick up pieces of dog dung, and eat it. We do the same. We try to fill up the emptiness inside with all sort of garbage. But garbage only fills the emptiness for a while; ultimately, it just makes the hole in the soul bigger.

People in America and throughout the world are so empty inside. They try to fill up the emptiness with any garbage they can. It might fill them for a second, but it does not fill them with anything lasting. I used to tell my students, who am I to tell you to stop sinning? I know that most of you will not listen. So I would be very sarcastic and say: So you think drinking will do it for you? Go ahead, drink until you puke. Do you think its sex? Oh yeah, go for it. Do you think it's money? Do you think it's power? Whatever it is, go ahead, go for it! I cannot stop you, and even God allows you to do it because He gave you free will. But I promise you, one day you're going to be lying in your bed. You might be alone; you might not be alone, but you are going to be empty as hell. When that day comes, I want you to remember this fat priest from Erie, Pennsylvania, and I want you to hear me say to you, "I told you so!" Nothing you ever have in this life will fill up the emptiness inside. Nothing. It might fill up for a second, or a minute or a day or even a year or years, but eventually it will leave you empty, I promise.

It's as if you have a bucket with a hole in it. You can put anything you want in it and it goes whoosh, right through. Money, whoosh, right through. Pleasure, whoosh, right through. Drink, whoosh, right through. Fill it up. Anything you want! Go for it! It's going to go right through. You might be happy for a moment, a day, a couple days, a couple years. But like I said, it's going to pass right on through and you're going to be empty.

The only thing that will fill up our emptiness is something that is eternal. The only thing that's eternal is God and His love. So when you try to fill up the emptiness with other things, you're going to stay empty. You are going to be a slave. However, when you fill it up with the love of God, you're going to have peace and freedom because now you're not concerned about yourself. You are whole and fulfilled. Now you can be more concerned about others. Now you can live a life of generosity. This is the exact opposite of what the world tells us, but it is the truth. Everything against the will of God only leaves us empty and makes the hole inside of us bigger. That's why you have to do it, whatever it is, again, and again, and again. Then what happens is that you become slaves to these things. You have to keep doing them again, and again, and again. But Jesus said, *Listen, you're a slave, but I've come to set you free!*

We celebrate Christmas because Jesus Christ became one of us. Why? To save His people from their sins! We read in Matthew 1:21, *She will bear a Son; and you shall call His name Jesus, for He will save His people from their sins.* The very reason Jesus became a man, the reason God became a man in the person of Jesus Christ, was to free us from our slavery to our sin — forever.

So first please fix your image of who God is, if it is a bad image. God is not like Joan Crawford in the book or movie *Mommy Dearest*. Remember that movie? One Christmas she went to her daughter's room and said, "Sweetheart, which of these presents do you like the best?" The girl said, "That one." Joan replied, "Well, that's the one that I'm going to give away! You can't have that one." We think God is like this. We think

He sits in heaven and asks, "What do you like to do the most? Do you like to have sex? Ha! You can't have that one! Whatever it is, you can't have it."

We really think that this is the way that God is. We think He has nothing better to do in eternity than to make us miserable. Then we develop a whole theology around why we're miserable, which says something like, "I'm miserable because God wants me to be miserable. I must suffer." Okay. Have fun with that.

The truth is that God came to set you free. Do you and I live in freedom, or do we live in slavery? By definition, a Christian should always have peace. Peace should be our regular state of being. Often when Jesus met the apostles after He rose from the dead, He'd say, *Peace be with you. This is my gift to you. My peace I leave you* (see John 20:26).

So, by definition, Christians should have peace in their hearts. If you don't have peace, it's usually because of one or two things. The first is because you're in sin. To have peace you need to repent of the sin. That is why one of the things I'm going to encourage you to do every day is to examine your conscience. It's a teaching of the Church that everybody, before they go to bed, should make a daily examination of conscience. If the Lord convicts us of any sin in our life we need to repent of it immediately and then ask for forgiveness, and if it is a serious sin get to confession as soon as possible.

If, after you have repented and gone to confession, you still don't have peace, then the second thing you look at is if you are doing the will of God. If you're not doing God's will, you aren't going to have peace. So that's what the rest of the book's going to be about — how to find out what you need do in order to do God's will. But for right now, we are going to focus on sin and repentance.

Sin, by definition, is doing things our way instead of God's way. This can be anything. It can even be good things if they are against the will of God. If we are doing something "because I've been brought up Catholic and I was brought up like this and this is the way my parents did it, this is the way I do it, and this is the way everybody's going do it," that's a sin. What if God asked you to do something different? "Well, He wouldn't," you might say.

Really? You do realize that the God of the Universe is a God of surprises, don't you? He loves to surprise us. He loves to come to us in ways we weren't expecting. Nobody expected Jesus Christ, the God of the Universe, to be born in a stable. Nobody expected Jesus Christ to be a suffering servant. Nobody expected the God of the Universe to die on the cross and suffer a horrible death. And yet God surprised us. We must always be is open to what God is calling us to next. We must be open to doing it His way and not our way.

That's a hard thing, because we get set in our ways. So the first thing when you do your daily examination is to walk through the day in your mind. Go through each thing with Jesus, every encounter you had with a person or on the phone and ask yourself this question, "Did they see me today or did they see Jesus today?" If the answer is that they saw me, then there is still a lot that needs to be repented. People are supposed to be looking and seeing Jesus in my life. So I need to ask if I'm pushing myself, and my ideas, or am I pushing Jesus and His ideas?

Remember, John the Baptist's desire was, *He must increase and I must decrease* (see John 3:30). John the Baptist humbled himself and exalted Jesus. That's what we've got to be doing, too, in our own lives. So if we aren't, we've got to repent for doing it our way instead of God's way.

When we make this daily examination, we've got to do more than just say, "I'm sorry," because sorry isn't enough now, is it? When I catch my dogs doing bad things (which is every day), they're sorry. My kids at Prep, when they did bad things (which again was every day), they were sorry when I caught them. They weren't sorry because they did it; they were sorry because they got caught. Isn't that what most people feel when they sin? "Okay, okay, I'm really sorry. I don't want to go to hell. I'm sorry. I won't do it again. Well, maybe I'll try not to do it again. How about that?" That's how we play this game with God.

To be forgiven of any of our sins, the number one thing that's necessary is repentance! Repentance is different than being sorry. When we try to discern God's will, we've got to be more than sorry for our sins. We've got to be repentant of our sins. Some people will say to me, "Now, Father, this is the only thing I struggle with, so it's no big deal." People of God, know this: It only takes one little thread to keep a bird from flying. Just one. So it is that one mortal sin in our lives can keep us from doing all God wants us to do. Just one habitual sin can keep us from being what God wants us to be. We have to really think about these things, don't we?

The Church has taught us that there are two kinds of sin, mortal and venial. Now some people think we make these things up. I know none of you think that, but some people do and so I say, "Do you really think we have nothing better to do than to make these things up?" Well, let us go back to the Word of God. 1 John 5:16, 17 says, *Anyone who sees his brother sinning, if the sin is not deadly should petition God and thus life will be given to the sinner. This is only for those whose sin is not deadly. There is such a thing as a deadly sin. I do not say that one should pray about that. True, all wrongdoing is sin, but not all sin is deadly.*

What is another word for deadly? Mortal. So, it's from Scripture that we get the difference between mortal sin and venial sin. Mortal sin kills our soul. Venial sin wounds our soul. When I was a kid in the '60s, I was taught by full-habited nuns. Sister told us, "Now, our souls should always be white. So, right when you go to confession, you get a pure white soul." Now this isn't the theology of the Church; it's just the way she explained it. She would say, "Now, if you commit a venial sin, it's like getting a little black spot on your soul. If you commit a mortal sin, it all goes black." I remember when I'd go to confession, and I went to confession a lot as a kid, I'd try not to run into anybody. I'd be thinking okay, there's no black spots on my soul now because I knew that as soon as I went into the house I'd get a black spot on my soul from fighting with my sister or brother or disobeying my parents. I had this image of me keeping a white soul with no black spots, and then I'd come home and my sister would say something to me and I'd say something back and then I'd think, "Oh no. Now I have a black spot on my soul."

Some people say, "It might be a sin, but it's only a venial sin." A venial sin wounds our relationship with Almighty God, so is it okay to wound your relationship with God just a little? Is it okay to say you love God, but you're okay with hurting Him? Remember, He always loves us. He does not get mad at us and say, "Okay, you've got a venial sin on you, and I don't want to talk to you." Or say, "Oh, you're a mortal sinner, so I don't love you." God is not like that.

Why treat sin as if it does not matter to God? Sin killed His Son, and so if we love Him, by His grace we need to kill sin in our lives, I have to deal with all the sin in my life, not just the mortal sin, but venial sin, too. I have to ask if I want to hurt the One who loves me more than anybody. Or do I want to do everything in my power to try to stop hurting the One who loves me more than anybody? That is the point.

We are all imperfect. Every one of us. We all need to go to confession. It's a good plan to go to confession once a month. When you go, please just don't pull out a list of things. You know, most people go to confession and it's the same old, same old. But God wants so much more. Instead of a list of things like, "I swore

237 times," think about entering into a relationship with Jesus. It is Jesus you encounter in the person of the priest, so when you come just tell Him why you're sorry for hurting Him.

As a priest, I love hearing confessions, especially when I'm on a mission and people haven't been to confession in 30 years or more. That's the average when I'm hearing confessions on a parish mission. If it has been 30 years since their last confession, I get all excited that they finally got enough courage to come home and receive the mercy Jesus is dying to give them. This is one of the greatest things about being a priest.

At the same time, there are some people who are very scrupulous and run to confession at the slightest hint of a sin. I get frustrated because they're often just so concerned about themselves. It is usually not about a relationship with Jesus. They are just concerned about their own holiness and whether they're good or bad.

That's a problem because it focuses on self. But let's say you do go to confession every week. If you go and talk about how you hurt Christ, well, that's an altogether different thing. You are not just going through a ritual of "Here are my sins. I made this list and I'm checking it twice." Instead you are saying, "Because I'm hurting you, Lord, when I talk about people I'm going to really stop doing that." Again, let me stress, repentance means I am not going to do it anymore. I am going to stop! Remember the traditional Act of Contrition? It says, "O my God, I am heartily sorry for having offended Thee. And I detest all my sins because of your just punishments. But most of all, because I have offended you, my God. . . ." See that? It's right in the prayer — "MOST OF ALL, BECAUSE I HAVE OFFENDED THEE." And then it goes on to say, I FIRMLY RESOLVE, with the help of your grace TO SIN NO MORE." Do you lie every time you say that? Because what you are saying is that you will sin no more. To "sin no more" has to be our intention when we go to confession. We have to say to Jesus, "I don't want to hurt you anymore."

We all have venial sins, the struggles we have day in and day out, the petty judgments we have in our lives, the gossips. But mortal sin, by definition, takes three things — serious matter, full knowledge, and full consent of the will. In other words, it's seriously wrong, you know it's wrong, and you do it anyway. If those three things are present, you're in mortal sin. You cannot go to Communion again until you have gone to confession. Now, let us deal with that for a second. Some people think a sin is just between me and Jesus. That is a very selfish way of looking at it. When you hurt Christ, you hurt everybody because, people of God, there is only one Body of Christ. Jesus is our Head. An analogy is that if you come and stomp on my foot, my whole body reacts. When you hurt Christ, you hurt the whole body. You hurt me, you hurt everybody else in the Church. When we hurt one another we also hurt Christ — that's why every sin is a communal sin.

In the early Church, there was no such thing as a private sin. In fact, in the early Church, after baptism there was no forgiveness of sin because there was no confession at that time. Baptism was the main way, and still is the main way, to forgive sins. Once a person was baptized, they could not be forgiven at all for any other sin. That is why a lot of people waited until their deathbed before they got baptized. They knew they couldn't live a lifetime without sinning.

The three big sins in the early Church were apostasy (to deny the faith, deny Christ), adultery, and murder. Many people fell into apostasy because of the threat of martyrdom. Many people were afraid of dying for their faith, so they would run away instead of being martyred. So the Church then said, "Okay, there is time for one forgiveness, one more time. God gave the power to the Church, so we'll forgive you once in your lifetime." That is the way it was in the beginning. Let's say you committed adultery, you murdered, or you committed apostasy. At the Sunday Mass, you would be brought into the church. You would then make a public confession to the whole body of Christ. People would say, "Oh, we all knew it, yeah, we did." Then a public penance would be given to you. You were not allowed back in the church until your penance was done.

What would happen next is you would stand out in front of the church wearing your hair shirt or doing whatever penance you were given, and as people walked in the church on Sunday, you would ask them to pray for you. That's where the penitential rite developed at the beginning of the Catholic Mass. It derived from the penitents outside the church asking to be prayed for before they were brought back inside. After you did your penance, you would be brought into the church, the bishop or the priest would come down, lay his hands on you, and forgive you in front of everybody. And then everyone had a great celebration.

Sin and forgiveness is always a communal thing. Always. The Irish monks made confession more private like we have today. Because there were so many people and the monks had only a limited amount of time, private confession was developed. Now you can have it the way it is today or you can go back to the way it was. Anybody want to go back to the way it was and make public confessions in church every Sunday? Wouldn't that be great? How come you are not laughing?

Isn't it interesting that forgiveness was not given until after the penance? That was the way it was in the Church from the beginning, but it's been changed to help us even more. However, what also happened was that we lost the communal aspect of sin. Remember, all sin is communal. All forgiveness is communal. So, if you've committed a mortal sin, such as missing Mass on Sunday, getting drunk on purpose, committing adultery, having an abortion, helping someone have an abortion, that hurts everybody, and you must be reconciled with God and reconciled with the Church.

How do we get free when we're struggling with sin again and again? The Word of God. John 8:31–32 says, *Jesus then went on to say to those Jews who believed in Him "If you live in my Word you are truly my disciples. Then you will know the truth, and the truth will set you free."* That's the key. If you live in my Word.

I don't know if you've ever read the *Confessions of St. Augustine*, but I love it. It's the greatest book because this saint was not afraid to show his sinfulness. He loved sex. He loved it. That is why he did not become a Christian for a long time. He was not willing to give up sex. He would say, "Lord, make me pure, but not yet."

Anyway, so he was a slave to his passions, but one day he's in the garden and he hears a voice say, "Take and read, take and read." He opens up the Word of God, and it falls to Romans 13:13–14: *Let us live honorably as in daylight, not in carousing and drunkenness, not in sexual excess and lust, not in quarreling and jealousy. Rather, put on the Lord Jesus Christ and make no provisions for the desires of the flesh.* As soon as Augustine read that, bang! Everything changed. He was free. What set him free, after all that struggling, after all that trying, was the Word of God.

So I encourage you, and I say it every time I talk, spend time with God in His Word. When you spend time with God in His Word, you will live life fully, and you will be set free. Take the holy Word of God and put it next to your bed. Every morning when you wake up, before you get out of bed, grab the Word of God, and pray to the Holy Spirit, "Spirit of the Living God, speak your Word to my heart." Then open the Word of God and read it until God takes a 2x4 and whacks you over the head.

Stop. Listen. Respond.

This will change your life and set you free, trust me.

Do you ever get depressed? Sometimes I do, because I get focused on myself or focused on what I'm doing. If you read the news first thing in the morning, it's always bad. Always. So you wake up and you're depressed. You go through the day being depressed. I ask you, why do you start your day with bad news? Why don't you start your day with good news, the holy Word of God? This is a great practice I talked about in the last chapter. To go further into this, I would encourage you to write down the Scripture verse that God spoke to you in the morning. Then put it in your pocket or your purse, and throughout the day pull it out, and read it. It will give you power because you are in a dialogue with God all day. The last thing you do at night, before you close your eyes, is to pray, "Spirit of the Living God, speak your Word to my heart," and again read the Bible that's waiting for you right next to your bed stand until God takes a 2x4 and whacks you over the head. After that, you let the Word of God take you to sleep at night.

Have you been struggling a lot with sin? Have you been a slave? I am giving you the remedy. Will you do it? That is the question. Most people never discipline themselves to do this. They talk a good game, but they won't do the simple, little things.

As always, our example is Jesus Christ. When Jesus was tempted by the devil in the desert, what did He do? Took the Word of God and shoved it down the throat of Satan and the devil ran. If that's how Jesus did it, people, that's how we're going to do it. If you don't, you're going to be a slave your whole life.

You want an example of discipline? Matt Talbot was an Irishman, born in Dublin, and he was a terrible, terrible alcoholic. By age 28, he would steal and do anyything else he could just so he could drink. But he would go to church on Sundays because he was a good Irishman. He said that even in his darkest days, he never lost sight of the Mother of God. At 28, when he had lost everything, he went to a priest and said, "I want to make a vow to never drink again in my life." And the priest said, "How about three months instead of your whole life?" He agreed, so he took that vow and he never broke it.

Now he's Venerable Matt Talbot. After Pope Paul VI read his life, Paul said this man must be a saint! In 1975 he was declared Venerable and he is going on to become this great saint of Almighty God, even though he had a very horrible life of addiction.

Many people are addicted to many different things. Sexual addiction is the number one addiction among men, but there's alcohol addiction, food addiction, all kinds of addictions that people stay in. The only thing that will set you free from your addiction is God. It's just that simple. So will you just stay where you are and make excuses, or will you come before Almighty God and let Him set you free?

One of my favorite stories is contained in *The Great Divorce*, by C.S. Lewis. In summary, it is a story about a man who struggles with lust his whole life. He has this demon on his shoulder that constantly makes him do horrible things. The man keeps crying out to God, "God, you've got to help me. God, you've got to help me." He keeps doing this until finally God sends an angel who asks, "What can I do for you?" The man replies, "I have this demon, this horrible demon that makes me do these horrendous things. I hate it." The angel looks at him and says, "May I kill it?" The man isn't sure, so he says, "Well, I don't know if I want you to kill it. Maybe you could wound it a little bit? You know, break its legs." The angel looks at him again and asks, "May I kill it?" And again the man says, "Oh, killing is not very politically correct. I don't know if you want to do that." The angel asks again, "May I kill it?" Finally the man says, "Yes, yes, kill it," so the angel reaches out and crushes the demon of lust. With that, the demon is transformed into a beautiful white stallion. The man jumps on the stallion and the stallion takes him home to heaven.

So it is with our own struggle. The God of the Universe looks at you and asks, "Do you want to be set free? May I kill your sin? May I kill your slavery? May I kill your addiction?" You've got to say, "Yes."

If we're going to discern God's will, we must be free of personal sin, or at least constantly repenting of personal sin because none of us is going to be free of it completely.

The next thing we need to do is make sure we live a life of forgiveness because Jesus was very clear about this throughout His teachings. In the book of Matthew Jesus teaches the people the Lord's Prayer and then He says, *If you forgive the faults of others, your Heavenly Father will forgive you yours. If you do not forgive others, neither will your Father forgive you* (see Matthew 6:14, 15).

There is no way you or I can do God's will if we do not forgive everyone who has hurt us. No excuses. No "everybody except for that one." God says if you forgive, then I will forgive you. If you do not forgive, then I will not forgive you. Every time you say the Lord's Prayer, you are saying, "Okay God, forgive me as I forgive." So, if you are very forgiving, great job. You have nothing to worry about. If you are not very forgiving — not good — I'd worry a lot.

If the God of the Universe will forgive you every day, how could you not forgive others? You might say, "Well, they hurt me." Well, you killed His Son. Every night you go before God the Father and say, "I'm sorry, please forgive me, I'm only human." Never once have I ever heard the God of the Universe say, "No, that's it; I've had enough of you." He's always willing to forgive you and He says now, though, you must go and forgive others.

Jesus teaches us this again in Matthew 5:23: *If you bring your gift to the altar and there recall that your brother has any-*

thing against you, leave your gift at the altar and go first and be reconciled with your brother and then come and offer your gift. If you and I are ever to discern God's will in our lives, we must be reconciled with our brothers and sisters. Reconciliation and forgiveness are not feelings. They are an act of the will. You have to think about that person, when they hurt you, and say to the Lord, "Lord, Jesus, I forgive them. And I ask you to forgive them." Once you do that, you are free. When you do not forgive somebody, do you do anything to them? No, you do not. You just continue to hurt and continue to stay a victim.

In counseling and in confession, people come to me and say, "Oh, Father, you know I was abused when I was a kid. That's why I'm the way I am." Shut up. You are the way you are because you have chosen to deal with it in this particular way. You like being a victim. So I say, "You are the way you are because you allow yourself to be victimized every day of your life. You've got to go back, forgive the person, and then move on with your life instead of sitting around for the rest of your life."

That does not sound very compassionate, does it? Oh, it is very compassionate, when they finally get set free, when they let go of this bitterness and this self-hatred and this holding on of everybody in this ugliness of life because of something that happened to them 30 years ago.

The best way to do this is to imagine that you and this person or persons are standing in front of the cross of Jesus Christ. As you are standing before the cross of Jesus Christ, He is bleeding and His blood is being poured out for you because He loves you. He has taken all your sins upon Himself as well as all the sins of that person who hurt you. Then Jesus takes His hand with the nail hole that you and I have put there, and He places it over your head, and His blood covers you and forgives you. Then imagine He takes that same hand and He places it over the person who hurt you and His blood forgives them and heals them.

You do not continue to walk in this slavery to your past. You need to let it go. If I have to say it harshly, I will, even if it makes you say, "I don't like you, Father." Do it anyway. Do it so you can experience the peace that Christ wants to give you. You can then walk in peace.

I want to be very clear — anything can be forgiven. I love to tell the story of an old friend of mine. He was a troubled youth. He became an alcoholic by the time he was 18, got a girl pregnant and married her. He liked to play cards. One day he was playing cards and he thought everybody cheated him because he lost, so he went home to get a gun to kill the people who he thought had cheated him in cards. His wife was eight months pregnant and she tried to stop him and so in his rage he killed her. He ended up in Rockview Penitentiary in Pennsylvania. He was there for a good many years. He always got in fights — once he spent 11 months in solitary confinement and another time 18 months. He was filled with hatred and hated himself. How could he not? He killed his wife and his eight-month-old child inside of her. A priest would sometimes stop by to see him and talk to him about the love of God and the forgiveness of God. He told the priest what he could do with his forgiveness, but the priest kept coming back to him. Finally, he opened him up to the Good News of the Gospel of Jesus Christ. He made a confession, and he started to change. He started to live in freedom. He became a model prisoner. His sentence was then commuted and he got out of prison. Now this guy's name is Brother James Townsend, O.F.M. He is a Franciscan brother and one of the most gentle men you could ever meet in your life. Yet, he is a murderer who killed his wife and his child.

God can give anybody freedom. Anybody. Once when I was preaching a men's retreat, a guy came in before confession started and cried, "Father, do you think God can forgive me?

Do you think God can forgive me?" Well, of course, God can forgive you . . . that's why He was born, and that's why He died.

No matter what your past has been, it doesn't matter. God can give you a new life if you surrender. See, that's the key to everything. A life of surrender means that I am a person who trusts completely, who surrenders my whole life, my whole past, my present, my future to the love of God. When I can do that, then I can forgive others because I've already given myself, I've already experienced mercy.

The problem is that a lot of people don't think they're that bad. I get that all the time when people come to confession. People say, "Well, Father, I didn't kill anybody." Let's look at that. According to Jesus, the worst sins are not sins of commission, but sins of omission. What we haven't been doing. How we have not been doing the will of God. How we haven't been taking care of the poor. How we have not been people of love. How we haven't been people of forgiveness. Those are the things that keep us bound and those are the things that Jesus Christ wants to set us free from.

I encourage you to make a daily examination of your conscience. When you do, don't pull any punches. Really just ask yourself, "Am I doing God's will or am I doing my own will?" Think about anyone you've hurt or been hurt by. If you've been hurt by anybody, always offer forgiveness in your heart first of all. If you've hurt anybody, go and be reconciled. Be reconciled. Write them a letter and say you're sorry. When you can do that, then you can start living the way God wants you to live. One of the greatest tools that God gives us to achieve the freedom that He promised us is His holy Word. So read the Bible. Keep it next to you every day. I have told people for years: "No Bible, no breakfast. No Bible, no bed." This means you do not eat breakfast in the morning until you have read from the Word of God, and you don't go to bed at night until you have read His

Word. It is there that you will receive the grace to be forgiven and the power to forgive others. It is in His Word that you will find the strength to stop sinning.

STEPS TO SURRENDERING YOUR LIFE

1. Begin making a daily examination of conscience, and develop this practice for the rest of your life. When the Spirit convicts you of your sin, repent and show God you are sorry.
2. Start the habit of monthly confession, unless you commit a mortal sin, then get to confession as soon as possible.
3. Be a person of forgiveness — forgive everyone who has ever hurt you.

A PRAYER TO HELP YOU ON YOUR WAY

Act of Contrition

Oh my God, I am heartily sorry for having offended Thee. And I detest all my sins because of Thy just punishments. But most of all, because I have offended thee, my God, who art all good and deserving of all my love. I firmly resolve, with the help of Thy grace, to sin no more and to avoid the near occasions of sin. Amen.

CHAPTER 4

Surrender and Be an Icon of Jesus!

"Sir, we would like to see Jesus." (John 12:21, NAB)

The one request every person who you meet every day makes of you, whether you are aware of it or not is: "Sir, or Ma'am, I would like to see Jesus." This is because a Christian needs to be another Christ. This means that Jesus lives inside of you and your job is to get out of the way and show people Jesus Christ. As we have seen earlier, a Christian is one who no longer lives for himself but lets Christ live inside of him (see Galatians 2:19). The purpose of a Christian, of course, is to be another Christ in the world. When it comes to discerning the will of God, we've got to make sure that we have the mind of Christ.

So often we're trying to discern with a physical mind or a fleshly mind, or a mind of the world. That kind of mind cannot discern the will of the Father; it just can't. We need to have the will and the mind of Jesus Christ if we're going to discern anything. You can always tell if something is from or not from God, because if it has to do with someone's personal opinion, it is not from God.

I can't tell you in the 20-plus years that I've been ordained how many people have said, "Well, Father, I know that this officially is a sin, but I think in my case God makes an exception because I've prayed about it. I have peace about it, and I really think . . ." They really mean it, and they go on and on! I always respond, "No, sorry, it goes against the Scripture. It goes against the teaching of the Church. You cannot be right. Absolutely you can't be right because you're looking at it with your own mind, or the mind of the world, or the mind of the flesh."

What has to happen if we're going to have the gift of discernment to know the will of God is that, with all our being, we have to try to have the mind of Jesus Christ. For that, you must spend time reading Scripture. In fact, I think you could spend every day for the rest of your life reading Philippians, Chapter 2. In verse two, Paul says to the Philippians, *Make my joy complete. By your unanimity, possessing the one love, united in spirit and ideals.* Then in verse three, he goes on, *Never act out of rivalry or conceit.* Now this is where it starts getting hard, because Paul says, *rather let all parties think humbly of others as superior to themselves, each of you looking to others' interests rather than your own.* This is the way Paul leads in to the Christological Hymn. He says, *Have the same attitude that is yours in Christ,* or as some translations say, *You must have the mind of Christ.* Or even, as an older translation puts it, *You need to have the attitude of Christ.* What does it mean to have an attitude of Christ? Paul explains it to us in verses 6–11:

> *Though he was in the form of God, Jesus did not deem equality with God something to be grasped at.*
>
> *Rather He emptied himself and took the form of a slave, being born in the likeness of men.*
>
> *He was known to be of human estate, and it was thus that He humbled himself, obediently accepting even death, death on the cross!*
>
> *Because of this guy, God highly exalted Him and bestowed on Him the name above all other names,*
>
> *So that at Jesus' name every knee must bend in the heavens, on the earth, and under the earth, and every tongue proclaim to the glory of God the Father.*

JESUS CHRIST IS LORD! There is enough to meditate on every day for the rest of your life in just those just few passages!

Another thing, when it comes to voting, I say, "If you just call yourself a Democrat or a Republican or an Independent, how sad that is! You are a follower of Christ who's going to vote in one way or another. Also, when you are going to vote, whatever it is, you need to vote as Christ would vote, correct? This is part of what it means to have the mind of Christ!

The big Christian fad about ten years ago was those little bracelets that read, "What Would Jesus Do?" Well, before we even begin to live "What Would Jesus Do," we have to first reflect on "What Would Jesus Think." To look at the world through the mind of Christ is very different from how the rest of the world thinks. It just is. But sometimes you cannot tell the difference between a Christian, a Catholic, or a pagan because they have the same mindset on everything.

Jesus said, *You're not of this world; my choice withdrew you from the world* (see John 17:14). So the question to ask when I am looking at life is, "Am I looking at things through the mind of the world, through the mind of the flesh, or am I looking at things through the mind of God?" The way you and I get the mind of God comes back to surrendering to the Holy Spirit.

Even when it comes to reading Scripture, if you read it with the mind of man, you may not get anything out of it. All kinds of people, even pagans, read the Scriptures all the time and don't get anything out of it. Why? Because when they approach the Scriptures, they approach them with a mind of a man, or with the mind of the world, or with the mind of the flesh. However, the only thing that can convey the Word of God, or the mind of God, is the Breath of God — the Holy Spirit. Let me explain. I cannot express to you what I am thinking when I am speaking unless my breath brings out my words to you. I could have all kinds of thoughts, but my breath brings out and conveys what I am thinking to you. Same with God. It's His breath that conveys His Word. And His breath is the Holy Spirit.

When we make any kind of decision, we have to really surrender ourselves to the Spirit of the Living God so that we can look at this through the mind of God, with the mind of Jesus, by the power of the Holy Spirit. This is very different than what most people do when they make decisions.

Often when I was teaching at the boys' school, I would ask a student, "Where are you going to go to college?" They would respond, "I don't know." I would continue, "Have you asked Jesus where He wants you to go?" "No." "Well, I think you should ask Jesus; it's going to affect the rest of your life and you should approach it with the mind of Christ. He already has a plan for your life, you need to ask Him what college that includes."

But most young people, when they're deciding what college they are going to go to are usually thinking about, "What major can I choose to get the most money? Where am I going to be partying the most? Where can I get the best girls or the best guys? Where can I get a husband or a wife?" That is how they're making their decision, instead of having the mind of Christ and saying, "Okay Lord, you created me for one thing. What do you want me to do with my life? What do YOU want me to do?" After that, put on the mind of Christ, which is so different than what 98 percent of the people in the world do. Most people make all their decisions with the mind of themselves or the world or the flesh, instead of with the mind of Jesus.

Every day we come before the Lord and say, "Okay, I want to have the mind of Christ." Now think about what that means — though He was in the form of God, He emptied Himself. So in order to have the mind of Christ I must have a life of service, as we talked about in Chapter 2. To live as Christ, to live your vocation, it must focus on love and service. So again, if God emptied Himself, then I'm going to empty myself. It's not about me; it's about what God's wanting me to do.

I remember one of my favorite verses of Scripture, which is in John's Gospel: *The world must know that I love the Father and do everything to please Him* (see John 14:31). The world must know that we love the Father with the mind of Christ, and that what I want to do is please Him.

It is a great thing to think about what you want people to say about you. One of the things I talk about in *Be a Man* is to "live with the end in mind," to think about what you want said about you at the end of your life by your family, your friends and, most importantly, by God. Do you want them to say you were good because you made a lot of money or you were great and powerful? Or to say you made a difference in the world? Think about this.

As I reflect on when I take my last breath, and I'm standing before the Father, I want to hear Him say, *Well done, good and faithful servant.* My purpose in life every day is to please the Father; to do what He wants me to do. But in my weakness, sometimes I do it well; sometimes I don't do it well at all. That is true of all of us.

Why do you wake up in the morning? To do the will of the Father? To please your Father in heaven? Or to go to work and make money, to get through another day? What is it? We need to have the mind of Christ. And, as I've said before, that comes from a surrender of your heart and your life to Him every day. *Lord, let me see things the way you see them today. Let me think about things the way you think about things today.*

One of the prayer practices in Catholic Tradition was that every morning you would say "The Morning Offering." Remember this prayer?

O Jesus, through the Immaculate Heart of Mary, I offer you my prayers, works, joys, sufferings of this day, in union with the Holy Sacrifice of the Mass throughout the world. I offer them for all the intentions of your Sacred Heart: the salvation of souls, the reparation for sin, the reunion of Christians; and in particular for the intentions of the Holy Father this month. Amen.

It was one way that you gave your whole life to the Lord each day. This is where it all begins, every morning offering everything that day to God!

This is reflected in the story of the Wise Men, or Three Kings, found in Matthew chapter 2. The Three Kings came before Christ, and the first thing they did was to prostrate themselves and do Him homage. They humbled themselves. So a good way to get the mind of Christ is to fall on your knees every morning. Every day, prostrate yourself the way the Kings did, and say, "Jesus, I love You, I give you my life, take over. . . ." Whatever it is you say, do this daily on your knees. When you do this, you are humbling yourself. And, as I've said many times before, you've got to do something that practical. This is something very practical, and you can start it tomorrow morning, so do it!

I tell people to do this at every mission I preach and so often, if I check back with people who made the mission, ninety percent of them won't have done it. They say, "I'm not getting on my knees every morning, are you kidding me?" A few will. A few will say, "Oh, yeah, you did say that, didn't you, Father?" Most people just think about it. See, I give very practical things. It's not like I preach la-la-isms such as, "Oh, just have nice thoughts about Jesus." NO! This is what you are going to do: you're going to FALL ON YOUR KNEES EVERY DAY. You're going to offer Him your treasure and give Him your gifts.

This gives us something practical to do. Sometimes we have to carry that out physically to have the mind of Jesus. When I fall on my knees every day, I make an act of humility. Jesus always made acts of humility. He left heaven for you and me. He took the form of a slave for you and me. He died for you and me. So when you wake up in the morning, after you get on your knees, you say, "Okay, Jesus, to have the mind of Christ, who do you want me to die for today?" Because He will call you to die today. (Aren't you excited?)

Every time you do the will of the Father, you are going to die. Every time. But do not get stuck on the dying part; you die so you can rise! It is when you die that you gain life. This is what Jesus did: When Jesus looked at the Father and said, "Your will be done," what did He do? He went to the Cross and died. When you and I say, "Your will be done," to the Father every day, sometime today God is going to let you die — out of love — because there is no love without sacrifice. If you love people, you are going to die for them — in little ways. For instance, there's only one piece of pie left in the refrigerator and you're starving, but you know your husband or wife wants it, or the kids want it, or your brother or sister wants it, and you say, "Okay, I'm not going to eat that piece of pie. I'm going to give it away." Or another example would be, let's say you're a man, you're watching TV, you're having your beer, and your wife comes walking into the room. You stop and look at her and say, "Oh, sweetheart, I love you," and hand her the remote control to the television and say, "We'll watch anything you want to watch tonight, sweetheart." That's a little way of dying. That counts for having the mind of Jesus.

It's the little things that we do. Going out of our way. Guys, you pick up flowers for your wife or, if you are a woman, when you make your husband's lunch, put a little "I love you" in there, a little card. It is the affirmations that make us think more about others than ourselves?

Just as a reminder, if we want to give up our lives every day to be with Jesus and to do things Jesus' way, the first thing we have to do is have the mind of Christ.

The next thing is we've got to act like Christ. This comes from 1 John 3:3, which says, *Everyone who has this hope based on him keeps himself pure, as he is pure*, or, as some of the new translations state: *Acts the way he acted*, or, *lives the way he lived*.

When I was a sophomore in college, I spent a summer working with a group called A Christian Ministry in the National Parks (ACMNP) in the Grand Canyon. I spent my whole summer there. This was an interdenominational group, and our ministry was to have ecumenical prayer services for vistors to the park on Sundays. Because I was a seminarian I was called to preach.

The very first homily I ever gave in the world was on Pentecost Sunday on the south rim of the Grand Canyon at a worship site. I had out my little homily all written out. I preached about how sin divides us, but the Spirit unites us. It was late in the afternoon, and if you have ever been to the Grand Canyon, you know it is beautiful. The sun was behind me and the first thing I said was, "Look at my stained-glass windows." Only about ten people were at those services and most people who came were Protestants. When I was done preaching one woman said to me, "Boy, that was a great Presbyterian sermon!" I said, "Well, I'm a Catholic seminarian." The poor woman almost had a heart attack and said, "Awwwww, Catholic, awwwww."

As I said, this was interdenominational ministry. We had Quakers and Baptists and we all worked together. First of all, the Quakers don't believe in sacraments. Quakers just believe in the spiritual sacraments and that kind of stuff. So, there was a woman by the name of Ruth; she was a great, great woman. Every time it rained we, the Catholics and the Baptists, would push her out in the rain and say, "We baptize you in the Name of the Father and the Son and the Holy Spirit," Just to make sure she was baptized!

One of the theological differences between Catholics and Baptists is that the Baptists believe it does not matter what you do because we are saved by Grace. Martin Luther would cry out, "Faith alone!"

Well, Catholics also believe that we are saved by faith, but not by faith alone. By God's grace, we need to live our lives the way Jesus did, because He should live through us. Years ago, I got into a debate with a guy who owned a big restaurant. He is an ex-Catholic and he would argue that all Catholics are going to hell and all such garbage. I would say, "Oh, stop it!" (As an aside, if you're into arguments like that, would you just grow up. Just grow up! If we all believe that we are saved by Grace we need to stop these petty arguments on just how and to whom this happens!) Anyway, this man would say, "It doesn't matter what I do." I looked at him once and said, "So, you go into McDonald's. You take a machine gun. You blow everybody away and kill them. You take the machine gun and blow your brains out. Are you going to heaven?"

"Of course, I am saved by Grace," he said.

Well I believe that that is a lie.

You need to surrender to Grace and live your faith if it is going to be real and effective.

We read in James 2:14–17: *My brothers, what good is it to profess faith without practicing it? Such faith has no power to save one, has it? If a brother or sister has nothing to wear and no food for the day, and you say to them, "Good-bye and good luck! Keep warm and well fed," but do not meet their bodily needs, what good is that? So it is with faith that does nothing in practice. It is thoroughly lifeless.* James, the brother of our Lord, goes on to say in verse 18–22, *To such a person one might say, "You have faith and I have works — is that it?" Show me faith without works and I will show you the faith that underlies my works! Do you believe that God is one? Oh, you are quite right. The demons believe that and shudder.*

Do you want proof, you ignoramus, . . . (I love that line — you know, these early saints were great in-your-face people.) . . . *that without works faith is idle. Was not our father Abraham justified by his works when he offered his son Isaac on the altar? There you see proof that faith was assisting his works and implemented by his works. You also see how the Scripture was fulfilled which says, "Abraham believed God and it was credited to him as justice"* for this he received the title *"God's friend."*

Now we come to verse 24: *You must perceive that a person is justified by his works and not by faith alone!* If we say we have the mind of Christ, that means we're starting to live as Christ. Now, again, everyone will bring forth a different face of Christ because Christ and His body (that's each of us) will bring forth a different reality of Christ.

I have a good priest friend who is a holy man (he makes me look like the greatest sinner there is). He was a campus minister at a coed school when I was campus minister at the boys' school. He would encourage kids by telling them that they are special. Isn't that nice?

I used to tell my boys at Prep, "Gentlemen, if you ever think I'm going tell you that you're special, it ain't going to happen."

When I would walk through the halls in the morning to go to say Mass, I would bump a student into a locker, and then I would move on and bump another youth (very gently, of course) into another and then ten of them would try to jump me and I would say, "You touch a priest, you go to hell forever."

That was my way, and the reality is that we each show a different face of Christ with our own personality. There is no one face of Christ. That's why we have the body of Christ. All of us are different — on purpose. So, what you must do is manifest the face of Christ as God lives it through you.

Each of the apostles was very different, were they not? Let us look at St. Peter and St. John; you couldn't get much different than Peter and John. Yet, each of them is a saint. St. Martha and St. Mary — each of them is a saint, but each showed a different face of God. And so it is. We can't go around thinking, "Well I do it better than anybody else." Or, "Look at me. I like my face as Christ better than Fr. Larry's face of Christ; that's not a very nice one." It's just a different one. There are people whom I can reach that many others cannot. There are other people whom other people can reach but I cannot. When I do a parish mission, I tell the people, "You know, I'm not here for the people who already know Jesus; I am here for the people who haven't been to Church in a long time, or the people who have been away from Confession for a long time."

Once I was preaching a big men's conference in the Midwest, and I had just given the Confession talk. When I am dealing with all men, I'm very different than when I speak in front of women. (Just as an aside, I think that Jesus dealt differently with His apostles than He did with other people.) So when I'm dealing with men I will say things that will make them think. I am into spiritual shock therapy, if you will, when I'm preaching to men. At the end of the Confession talk, I will say, "Suck it up, go to Confession. It's time. Those of you who are wimps and have never been to Confession in 30 years — it's time. Jesus is waiting." And so there are always big lines to the confessionals. I'm into this real theology stuff — none of this la-la-la-la-la. Men don't respond to la-la; they just don't. Most men don't, anyway. Anyway, it was at the end of the talk and I had to leave so I could only hear a few Confessions. The guy who was in charge, Hector, called me a couple days later and he said, "Oh, Father, great, great response to your talk. It was so good. People did a lot of writing about how they loved your talk, but I've got to tell you, one guy came up to me and asked, 'So, what'd you think of Fr. Larry's talk?'" Hector continued, "I said, 'Oh I liked it,' but the other guy said, 'I think he should be defrocked. He should be thrown out of the priesthood. Did you hear what he said in the presence of the bishop?'"

Hector told me about how this guy was going on and on about how I should be thrown out of the priesthood and how he was going to write a letter to the bishop. Well, as Hector is talking, I'm thinking, "The Bishop says the biggest file of hate mail he has on any priest in the diocese is about me, so just join the crowd." Anyway, Hector said he asked the guy, "Well, do you really think Fr. Larry should be put out of the priesthood?" The guy said, "Yeah." So Hector told me he said, "Just turn around." The guy turned around. "What do you see?" Hector asked him. "Guys going to Confession." "That's right," Hector said he told him. "Thousands of guys going to Confession. We have never had this many people go to Confession before. That's why Fr. Larry's a priest."

Different people do different things. That is the whole point: You are going to be different than I am. You are going to be different than your husband or your wife or your children. Your children are not called to be in your image, are they? Sometimes people think they have kids so kids can be in their image. Excuse me — they're not — they're to be in God's image. That's the point.

We're all called to bring the face of God to the world. When we are discerning "What does God want me to do," we have to recognize that we need to be Christ in the world. When we are discerning, "What does God want me to do?" we need to ask, "How does He want me to be His son or His daughter," if you will, "in the world?" The world wants to see Jesus; people do not want to see me. Remember the words of John from the beginning of the chapter, *Sir, we would like to see Jesus*, and show people Jesus Christ.

My favorite verse in the Bible is Galatians, chapter 2:19–20:

*I have been crucified with Christ. So the life I have now is
no longer my own. Jesus Christ lives inside of me. I still live my
human life, yes, but it's the life of faith in the Son of God who
loved me and gave His life for me.*

This is the core of what it means to follow Jesus. We must
die. It's what has to happen for us to be transformed into Christ.
If you have not died, you have not yet become a follower of
Christ. As I have said again and again, to follow Christ it must
cost you your life every day. What you're called to do and what
I'm called to do is to show people Jesus. So now that we know
this, we need to live this.

I love the story of the man who was captured in World
War II and thrown in a Japanese prisoner-of-war camp. He was
treated badly, but not as badly as another guy, a Japanese who
was trying to help the Americans. The captors tortured the
Japanese man every day and deprived him of food. Every day,
he would be thrown into the same cell as the American, and
every day the American would take his own food and give it
to the Japanese man and try to heal his wounds as best as possible.

One day they had tortured the Japanese man so badly that
when they threw him back in the cell with the American, the
American knew that he was going to die. So he knelt next to
him, and said, "You know, you're probably going to die tonight.
But you don't have to be afraid. If you just give your life to Jesus
you will live forever."

You know what the Japanese man said to the American? He
said, "If this Jesus is anything like you, I can't wait to meet him."

Could people say that about us? Could your husbands say
that about you, ladies? "Oh, sweetheart, if Jesus is anything like
you, I can't wait to meet him." Husbands, could your wives say
that about you? "Oh, honey, if Jesus Christ is anything like you,

I can't wait to meet him." Could your children say that about you? Could your parents say that about you? Could they say, "If Jesus Christ is anything like you, I can't wait to meet him."

To get the mind of Christ, and to live the life of Christ in the world today will cost you your life. But then you get to show the world Jesus. What a life!

Now, of course, this is all a lifelong process and we'll each do it in a different way. We'll have our strengths, we'll have our weaknesses, and that's okay. But the point is that you and I are trying to die more and more to ourselves so that others may see Jesus more and more.

One saying often attributed to St. Francis is: "Preach the Gospel at all times and, if necessary, use words." This means that the way we are living speaks so loudly that it really does not matter what we're saying.

This is an issue with my own ministry, too. I can say some wonderful things and I can write them in wonderful ways, but when I go home I think, "Boy, if I just lived what I preached I would be a saint, but that is the problem; I do not always live it!" What has to happen is every day, little by little, we must be transformed and allow ourselves to be instruments of God and allow Him to take over and have full control.

That is why there is always the fight inside of us — to do God's will or to do our will — because it will cost me my life to do God's will. Now remember that Christ is resurrected. He's no longer on the cross. We keep images of Him on the cross to remind us of His death. We preach Christ crucified, and we say that He suffers still in all of us, but He's alive, and we must also focus on this great reality.

Some people like to spend their whole lives focusing only on the cross. I think that's morbid. We must go through the cross, but not stay there.

I am an Easter person, not a Lent person. Lent is when we focus on dying to self. Some Catholics can get a little crazy because they love Lent a little too much. They love to brag: "I can't eat meat today or I gave up chocolate and I gave up this." They can be all proud about it. That's why I love to challenge people by telling them, "I want you to live Easter." The Church does the same thing. The Easter season is longer than the Lenten season. Yep, the Easter season lasts 50 days, but Lent lasts only 40.

St. Augustine said, "We are an Easter people." So, although you must die, you don't have to stay dead. You resurrect every time you and I give our lives away. We get something better out of it! When you say, "I'm going to give my life away in service," the God of the Universe will give you even more back.

When I was ordained in 1988 as a deacon, on October 15, the feast of the Carmelite Teresa of Ávila, the Mother Superior of the Carmelites near me said, "Well, Father, you need to be ordained on a strong woman's day because you need a strong woman in your life. St. Teresa of Ávila is one of the strongest woman saints we have."

In Chapter 2, I talked about how the kids at the youth conference gave me a medal that I still have with an inscription that reads, "Larry's Kids" on the back. At the time I thought I was giving up everything when I chose to be celibate, but God had met my need and gave me even more. He blessed me even more abundantly with children than if I would have had just the ten kids that I wanted. Father's day is one of my biggest days. I could have been the father of a few, but God called me to be the spiritual Father of many! So don't focus on the cross; just focus on going through the cross. Do not focus every day on, "I've got to die and I have to enjoy it." Die and experience the life you will get when you do it.

If any of you have ever been involved in ministry I bet you have had the experience of thinking, "You know, I got more out of this than I gave today." Once I was in a parish in south-western Pennsylvania doing a mission. I was complaining as I do about how busy I am and that always seemed to be doing something and I'm always giving, giving, and giving. As I was complaining to the associate priest of the parish, he just looked at me and said: "Isn't it great, Father, that our tiredness brings refreshment to others?" I just wanted to say, "Oh, shut up." But it is so true. I was focusing on myself instead of focusing on all the people who were being refreshed by me giving away my life. And that's what we've got to do. When we have the mind of Christ, instead of thinking, "Oh, I'm tired from all the things I'm doing," we look at others and think, "Boy, that person's refreshed, that person's forgiven, that person has a new life! Wow — isn't it a glorious thing!"

What will help us grow the most is spending time with Jesus in His Eucharistic Presence. The most important thing for me, and it's always been, even before I was ever ordained, is Mass. The Church teaches that the Mass, or the Eucharist, is "the source and summit of the Christian life" (CCC 1324). As Catholics we are so blessed to be able to receive Jesus in the Eucharist. You know the old saying: you become what you eat. The more you eat of Jesus, the more you become Jesus. For those who are reading this and who do not believe that Jesus is really present in the Eucharist, I just want to encourage you to open yourself to the truth that when Jesus said, "This IS My Body" and "This IS My Blood," that Jesus Christ is NOT A LIAR! The Church has taught this truth from the very beginning. You can believe Jesus and His Church. Ask the Holy Spirit to lead you — He will — Jesus promised, *When He comes, however, being the Spirit of truth, He will guide you to all truth* (see John 16:13). On the last night of a parish mission, I'll look at the tabernacle and ask, "How many people really believe that Jesus Christ is present there?" Everybody will raise their hands and I say, "Whoa, I'm impressed." Then I will ask, "How many of you go to Daily Mass?" About ten percent of the people, or five percent of the people, or just one percent of the people, raise their hands. I look at everybody else and I say, "The rest of you are liars." They look at me and I can tell they are thinking, "Why don't you die right now, Father. We really don't like you. Just drop dead. All you do is make me feel guilty."

So I go on, "Excuse me. What did Jesus teach us when He taught us to pray? It's *give us this day our daily bread.* Not our weekly bread, our daily bread" (see Matthew 6:11). Jesus Christ, who is the God of the Universe, is present here in the Eucharist. It is here in His Eucharistic Presence that He fulfills His last promise, *Know that I am with you always, until the end of the world* (see Matthew 28:20). He wants to feed you with His own Body and Blood, and all you do is give Him excuses of why you don't have the time to go to Mass. So I go on and then ask, "What if I told you I'd give you a million dollars if you would go to Mass every day for the whole year. I'll bet you'd make it to Mass every day. Well, here you're getting more than a million dollars. You're getting the God of the Universe who will humble Himself before you." He makes you one of the greatest promises that He could ever make when He tells us, *He who feeds on My Flesh and drinks My Blood has eternal life and I will raise him up on the last day* (see John 6:54).

So it comes down to this: "Do you want to be with Jesus? He wants to be with you, and He proves it by waiting for you each day. He wants to become one with you in the intimacy of His Eucharistic Presence. So I'd encourage you, if you don't have a habit of Daily Mass in your life, try to develop one. If you cannot do it immediately, go once a week, twice a week, then three times a week, and then four times a week. If you do that, you will learn that it becomes part of your life, part of your prayer life. For some of you it will be very difficult. But as I have said before, "What do you wake up for in the morning? Do you wake up for money or do you wake up for Jesus?" So for some of you to get to Mass, you will just have to wake up earlier. Isn't it a great thing to sacrifice for Jesus? If it's hard for you to wake up in the morning — so what? Do it for Jesus.

You might be thinking, "Well, now Fr. Larry's got me falling on my knees in the morning, reading the Word of God in the morning, and going to daily Mass. What does He want me to be, a saint?" Yes, as a matter of fact, that's what I want and what God wants and that's what we must become. We must become Christ in the world. If we spend time with the Scriptures every day, if we are going to Daily Mass, then we have a heart that is seeking God's will. So, I'd encourage you to go to daily Mass, and to visit an adoration chapel if your parish has one, because when you just sit with Jesus present there in the Blessed Sacrament for an hour, you become changed.

Let me give you an analogy. Let's say it is one of those days when the sun is out and you go to the beach. All you have to do is lay there. The more naked you are, the more you will be transformed, correct? So if you are there and you're under an umbrella, not much is going to happen because you're covered. But if you're there and you're in your bathing suit, under the sun, then things are going to change. The more exposed you are, the more you get changed by the rays of the sun. When you come into the presence of Jesus, you get a "SON" tan and are transformed by Him. Slowly you and He become one.

Now I know it's impossible for some people to go to daily Mass, and I realize some parishes don't have adoration chapels, so if you can stop at the church every day before or after work. My grandmother was a great woman. She had a ditty that went:

> Every time I pass a church,
> I stop and make a visit,
> So when the time comes

> When I'm wheeled in,
> He won't say, "Who is it?"

At the end of your life, when Jesus asks you, "Do you want to be with me forever?" you want to be able to answer, "Yes, Lord, that's why I spent time with you in the Scriptures; that's why I always spent time with you in the Blessed Sacrament." So He will then look at you and say, "You have proven to me you just want to be with me. Now I will give you myself forever." The way we live every day is how we'll live for eternity.

To become Christ in the world, we're going to have to die to ourselves. We are going to have to get His mindset, and then we must become Christ to the world. We do that best through receiving the Eucharist and spending time with Him each day. Got it?

STEPS TO SURRENDERING YOUR LIFE

1. Daily Bible
2. Daily Mass
3. Daily offering
4. Eucharistic Adoration

A PRAYER TO HELP YOU ON YOUR WAY

Prayer of Transformation

Lord, take my hands. I give them to you so you may continue to bless, to heal, work, feel, comfort, and love. Forgive me for using them for things against your will.

Lord, take my mouth. I give it to you so you may continue to speak, preach, build up, comfort, and love. Forgive me for all the times I have hurt you and your people with my mouth.

Lord, take my nose and my senses. I give them to you so you may continue to sense good from evil, and smell the fragrance of your love in all people. Forgive me for distorting this for my own will.

Lord, take my eyes. I give them to you so you may continue to see the good in all men, the Spirit of your Father, the Spirit of your love. Forgive the times I have seen only the evil and then judged.

Lord, take my ears. I give them to you so you may continue to listen and hear the cry of the lonely. Forgive me for all the times I have closed them, closed them to your Truth.

Lord, take my feet. I give them to you so you may continue to lead myself and others in the path of your love. Forgive me for using them to follow a path of selfishness.

Lord, take my body. I give it to you so you may continue to suffer so as to carry on my dying to myself. Forgive me for wanting to use it for the desires of the flesh.

Lord, take my mind. I give it to you that I may think the way you think. Forgive me for so often thinking with the mind of the world or the flesh.

Lord, take my heart. I give it to you so you may continue to love and understand. Forgive me for all the times I have let my heart be hardened.

Lord, take my life. I give it to you so you may continue to live through me. Forgive me for wanting to only live for myself.

Lord, I give you my very self. Everything. All that I am. Just as I am. I give myself to you so that your will and not mine may always be done in me.

Amen.

— Fr. Larry Richards

CHAPTER 5

Surrender and Hear God's Voice!

"My sheep hear my voice; I know them, and they follow me." (John 10:27, NAB)

To know God's will we must listen to His voice. Throughout the years people have called me for advice, asking, "Father, what should I do? What is God's will for me?" I always answer the same thing — PRAY! They usually respond, "I knew you were going to say that!"

People do not want to be told that if they want to know God's will they should pray. It is too simple for them. They usually say, "Father I have been praying and I did not hear anything." I just tell them they have to "shut up when you pray." Just shut up! But you see to "shut up" means you are going to have to hand over control to God. (I know that some of you are thinking that I should not use the words "shut up," but I am trying to make a point here — are you getting it?)

You are going to have listen to fully surrender.

God commands us in His Word: *Be still and know that I am God* (see Psalm 46:11). This is absolutely necessary if you are ever going to hear God and come to know His will. However, being still when you pray takes time and patience. As God tells us through the prophet Isaiah: *For thus says the Lord God, the Holy one of Israel: By waiting and by calm you shall be saved, in quiet and in trust your strengths lies* (see Isaiah 30:15). This means you need to wait upon the Lord when you pray. You are not in charge — He is.

In 1 Kings 19:11, God spoke to the prophet Elijah, *Go up into the mountains and there I will speak to you.* Elijah goes up to the mountain and what happens? *A strong and heavy wind came.* Was God in the strong, heavy wind? No. An earthquake comes. Was God in the earthquake? No. Then a fire comes. Was God in the fire? No. And then *a tiny whispering sound* (v. 12) came and Elijah hid his face because now God was present.

Elijah had to wait for the Lord. He didn't say, "I have been here ten minutes and nothing is happening and so I am leaving." He did not say, "This is a 'sign' but not the one I wanted so I am out of here." He stayed there until he heard God's voice.

If you are going to discern the will of God in your life, you need to be patient, you need to listen and you need to commit yourself to prayer. Prayer is the only way you can hear God's voice. The only way. Too many people come to me and say, "Father, I asked God for a sign." They are looking for "signs" instead of looking for God! Do you see what is wrong with that?

People look to St. Thérèse, the Little Flower, and say, "Send me a rose," because she has been known to send roses in answer to prayer. Then they go crazy when they get a rose or despair if they do not get one. The problem is that they are looking at this as magic or superstition because it is about them instead of being about God. I think that God's response to a request for a sign sometimes is just, "Shut up and stop looking for a sign. Just be with me and wait for me and I will tell you what you need to know." People respond, "Well, no, I want a sign."

Now God does use signs sometimes. God sent an angel to Gideon telling him, *The Lord is with you, O champion!* (see Judges 6:12). The angel then told Gideon that God wanted him to destroy certain people. Gideon asked, *Who am I?* and then he said he wanted a sign. He put out a fleece, saying if in the morning it was wet with dew and the ground was dry, he would know it was God's will. He got that sign — the fleece was wet and the ground was dry. But Gideon wanted another sign. This time, he wanted the ground to be wet and the fleece to stay dry. And again, in the morning, he got that sign.

So God does give signs, but looking for them is not an act of trust in God. It is about my wanting to see what all my options are and making sure I'm right, instead of having a relationship of love. So instead of asking for signs when you want to know God's will, I hope that first of all you come to know that God loves you more than you can ever love yourself and that He wants what is best for you. You can trust Him with your life.

He is your Father. He is your Dad. He created you out of nothing. He had a plan for you before you were ever born. He already knows the end of your life, and your job is to trust Him more than yourself.

The only way to get to know God is to spend time with Him. The only way to get to know His voice is to listen to Him when you are spending time with Him in silence every day. You need to have silence in your prayer. If you do not incorporate silence in your daily prayer time, it is not going to happen. It has to be a discipline in your life.

Hopefully, you will spend at least 10 minutes a day in prayer. I know you are very busy, but St. Francis de Sales said, "Everyone needs at least one half hour of prayer every day, except of course if you are busy — then you need an hour!"

Now, I am not going to tell you that you have to spend a half-hour or an hour in the beginning, but you can start with at least ten minutes. Five minutes is spent doing your talking and your prayers and then five minutes in stillness and listening to God and letting God speak to you and love you. This takes discipline.

So the first thing you need to do when you come into God's presence is to make an act of surrender: "Lord, I surrender myself to You and to Your will."

Now, this is something you do automatically when you say the Lord's Prayer. This is usually the only penance I have given throughout my priesthood. It is always the same — "Say one Our Father." People look at me and say "Oh, Father, that is not enough." I answer, "It is the perfect prayer of Christ. If it is not enough, then I can't give you anything else." Sometimes, they say, "Give me ten Our Fathers or give me a rosary, Father. I will feel better." I tell them, "I am not the least bit interested in making you feel better. I am asking you do the penance that I as the priest have given you. You say one Our Father. You say it slowly and you mean every word and that will be a big enough penance for the rest of your life."

I usually encourage them to spend time on two phrases of the Lord's Prayer. First, the word "Father." What does it mean to be a beloved child of God? St. Teresa of Ávila could not say the Lord's Prayer with being caught up into ecstasy. As soon as she started saying "Our Father" she would go into ecstasy for hours. She would be in ecstasy over the thought of what it means for the God of the Universe to be her dad.

Second, I tell them to spend time with the phrase, "Thy will be done." When you spend time with those words, you are telling God that whatever He wants is what you want. What most people means when they say the Lord's Prayer is: "Our Father who are in heaven hallowed be Thy name, Thy Kingdom come, 'MY' will be done on earth as it is in heaven!"

Sometimes people come, and say, "Father, I am mad at God." When I ask why, they respond, "Because I have been praying for something for the last four months and I have not gotten it." I say, "Oh, that's prayer? 'Hey, You, God of the Universe, jump through my hoop. Here it is, and if you don't, I'm mad at you.'"

Prayer is not to conform the will of God to our will. Prayer is about confirming our will to the will of God. The greatest example of this is Jesus praying in the garden of Gethsemane, "Not as I will but as you will." When you say, "Thy will be done," you are really saying, "Whatever you want I want and I am grateful for, God."

I know I am not the most gentle of people, so when someone comes to me and says, "Father, I am having a bad day," I usually say, "Did you thank God for your bad day?" If they say, "No," I respond, "Did you say the Lord's Prayer this morning?" If they say, "Yes," then I continue, "Did you say, 'Your will be done'? If you did, then this is His will for you. Why are you not thanking Him for it? That is what you asked for — His will for you. He gave it to you and now you are mad?"

When you and I say, "Your will be done," that means everything in our lives today, except for sin, which is going against the will of God in our life, will be God's will for us. So at the end of the day, even if it is a miserable day, you can say, "Thank you. Your will was done in my life today. I didn't like it, but thank you. It is what I asked for today." Priests and religious say this every night before they go to bed when they say night prayer, when they pray the canticle of Simeon: *Lord, now you let your servant go in peace; Your word has been fulfilled. My eyes have seen the salvation You have prepared in the sight of every people, A light to reveal you to the nations and the glory of your people, Israel* (see Luke 2:29–32). This is traditionally called the *Nunc dimittis*, which is its first two words in Latin. No matter how the day went, we thank God that we have seen His will and His salvation!

When it comes to His will, God makes us some promises in His Word. If you read Romans 8:28, God tells us, *We know that all things work together for the good of those who love Him who have been called according to His decree.* He won't make His will or make everything work out good for everybody. He will only make it work out for good to those who give Him charge over their lives, only those who surrender to His will.

If you want to do it your way, then God will let you be god of your own life. He says, "I love you. If you want to be in charge of your life, I will let you be in charge of your life." That means when horrible things happen, don't blame God because you are god of your own universe. You have not surrendered to Him. You are your own god. See how that works? When you surrender everything to the Lord every day, then the Lord can do great things for you.

When I was a sophomore at Gannon University, I was already in seminary. At the time I went through a great depression. I was so depressed that my eyebrow would start to twitch uncontrollably at times. I would go to class sometimes, but a lot of times I would not even come out of my room. I would spend nights upstairs on the third floor of the seminary in front of the Blessed Sacrament in a small chapel. It got so bad that I did not even go home one spring break, but went on a silent private retreat at a retreat house.

The only thing I did was to eat once a day. The rest of the time I would spend in the chapel. To help me through this, I would repeat the same prayer over and over again. I did not just go through the motions with this prayer, but I said it with my whole being with a great intensity.

It was the prayer of Venerable Charles de Foucauld. He was a hermit who founded the Little Brothers of Jesus, but he was also man who had great excesses in his early life. An agnostic, he had great parties and a great time with women before he came to a great conversion. After that, he wanted to spend his life with the hidden Jesus, so he moved to Nazareth and spent the time as a hermit. He worked with the Arabs and died among them. One of his prayers is the prayer that I said every day. I said it many times during those days when I was so depressed.

> Father,
> I abandon myself into your hands; do with me what you
>   will.
> Whatever you may do, I thank you:
> I am ready for all, I accept all.
> Let only your will be done in me, and in all your creatures.
> I wish no more than this, O Lord.
>
> Into your hands I commend my soul;
> I offer it to you
> with all the love of my heart,
> for I love you, Lord,
> and so need to give myself to you,
> to surrender myself into your hands,
> without reserve,
> and with boundless confidence,
> for you are my Father.

I just kept saying that prayer in the midst of my depression: "I abandon myself. . . . I accept all . . . surrender myself in your hands . . . for you are my Father." I remember praying this repeatedly in front of Jesus in the Blessed Sacrament. It was the darkest place I have ever been. It was as if I had reached the bottom of my soul. One of the things I found out as I was praying this prayer was that I was not alone. God was there and He was my Father. I thought to myself, I can handle this because I am not alone. I got out of the depression instantly. That doesn't normally happen, but it happened to me.

This prayer helped me to surrender finally to His will. When you abandon yourself, the Lord will take care of you. Maybe not instantly, but He is going to take care of you because He has to.

He is your Dad and He loves you more than you love yourself. Surrender every day, give yourself to Him, hand over to Him the control of everything. He will do the rest. Trust Him.

I try to get people to do this surrender in our Adoration Chapel at my parish. Throughout the years, I always wanted an adoration chapel. When I became pastor of St. Joseph Church Bread of Life Community, one of the first things I did was build an Adoration Chapel and start Perpetual Adoration. On the wall of the chapel is the command of God: "Be still and know that I am God." (It could have said, "Shut up and know that I am God," but that is not very gentle.) The phrase is to remind people that when they enter the chapel they are not just to fill up their time with all their words, and all their thoughts and all their concerns, but they are encouraged to let God love them and hold them and just be with them.

So when you are going through all your crazy times, He will help you through those times. If you can just breathe, be still, and surrender and know that He is God, then everything will go into perspective. The saints used to say, "What is this compared to eternity?" When you have the perspective of eternity, you can look back and think about it, that 100 million years from now, we are going to be alive. We may even ask each other, "Remember that time on earth when we were going through that struggle where we had a hard time when we were depressed?" and we are going to look at each other and say, "No, I don't remember that. It is a distant memory."

When you and I go into the presence of the God, we get to experience eternity while we are still here. We get into the "now-ness" of God and the rest of our struggles are put into perspective of "This too shall pass." It will. But we have to make sure that we have a committed time in our lives.

In the Office of the readings for the feast of St. John Vianney, we read a passage from his catechetical instructions. He states:

"Some men immerse themselves as deeply in prayer as fish in water, because they give themselves totally to God. There is no division in their hearts. Oh, how I love these noble souls! St. Francis of Assisi and St. Colette used to see our Lord and talked to Him just as we talk to one another. How unlike them we are! How often we come to church with no idea of what to do or what to ask for. And yet, whenever we go to any human being, we know well enough why we go. And still worse, there are some people who seem to speak to the good God like this: 'I will only say a couple of things to You, and then I will be rid of You.' I often think that when we come to adore our Lord, we would receive everything that we ask for, if we would ask with living faith, and with a pure heart."

What he is saying is that we need to spend time with God and be with him like any other relationship! This is not about ritual alone; it is about friendship with Jesus!

If only we knew how much we are loved by God! Too many people look at prayer as a burden. We think it is something we have to do to be a good person. Or we think "Father Larry says I have to pray every day." You should pray because you want to be with the One you love. More so, you should pray because you want to be with the One who loves you.

When I was younger, I used to go home to Pittsburgh about once a month, and as I would come walking in the house my sister would say, "Uncle Larry is here." And My little niece Samantha, who was about two or three years old at the time, would drop whatever she was doing and come running to me. I would grab her and lift her up and hold her close to my face and hug her and say, "Oh, hugs, hugs, hugs." She would put her little head next to mine and squeeze me tight and say, "Ah." She would not move for 10 minutes. She would just cling to me because she knew how much I loved her.

That is prayer! Every day your Father calls you by name. Every day. He calls you by name and the only thing He wants to do is embrace you and hold you. When you go to prayer you are in the arms of your Father. The deepest need in all of our hearts is to be loved — period. God wants to fill that need every day. So when we go running to Him, He embraces us, holds us and loves us. Why would you not want to pray when you know that is what is happening there?

Our job is to go running to Him and stay with Him. When we are saying our prayers God says, "Yes, I know all this already. Now can I hold you?" and you respond. "No. I am done. I have to hurry up and get to work or go get . . ." And God responds, "Okay." We just run out and God says, "I could not even hold you." He wants to hold you.

Now some of you are going to be a little freaked out about being that intimate with God, but what I am calling you into is "spiritual childhood." Remember Jesus told us, *I assure you, unless you change and become like little children, you will not enter the Kingdom of God* (see Matthew 18:3). This is where it all began with Jesus and this is where it must begin with you! At His baptism God the Father looked at Jesus and said, *You are my beloved Son, with whom I am well pleased* (see Mark 1:11). So get over yourself, and become a spiritual child!

There are some people who focus on the mechanics of prayer instead of the relationship part. For example, some people come to me and say, "Oh, Father, I was distracted in prayer." I say, "Oh stop it, don't focus on the distraction, just be in His Holy Presence. When you are holding a baby, do you care if the baby is sleeping, or playing with your nose or picking your ears or pulling your hair? No, the baby wants to be with you and that is okay."

In my own life there are times that I am so tired and I fall asleep, especially if it is a late night and I just got off the road and I might have not yet said Mass or done my holy hour and I just say, "I am sorry, Lord." Do you think the Lord gets mad because I fell asleep in His arms? I don't think so. As long as you want to be with Him, that is what He wants.

If you are going to be faithful, figure out times in your day for daily prayer. Realize it must be consistent. I don't care when you do it, but what I find most practical when I am dealing with people in spiritual direction is to decide to give a certain amount of time to God every day. So instead of deciding that every morning you will pray from 5:15 to 6:00, you say, "Lord, every day I will give you this much time." So if you have to skip prayer in the morning because something else happened, you give it to the Lord later in the day.

Years ago I was sitting before Jesus in the Blessed Sacrament in Franciscan University of Steubenville at their in Perpetual Adoration Chapel. I remember looking at Jesus and saying, "Jesus, I promise you for the rest of my life that I will give you one hour a day in prayer no matter what." And I have never broken that promise. I have not always been able to do it in front of the Blessed Sacrament as I like to, but He always gets the hour, period.

I have done this for at least the last 25 years because that was the promise I made to Him. Sometimes it is at one o'clock in the morning, but He gets the hour because I told Him I would give Him the hour. Once I was in Denver when Pope John Paul was there. I had taken my youth group along with our diocese and our bishop to see Him. It was late at night. I made sure all the kids were in bed, and then I was going to say Mass and do my Holy Hour. The bishop saw me as I was going outside of the hotel and asked, "Where are you going?" I said, "I have not done my Holy Hour yet, Bishop, so I am going to go out to say Mass and do my Holy Hour." The bishop looked at me and said, "Oh, Larry, I could dispense you from that." I replied, "Bishop, I did not make the promise to you. I made it to God." And he let me go. He understood. (I have a great bishop!) I went out, did my Holy Hour, and said Mass. It was similar to the promise I made to the Bishop when I promised him obedience and respect and celibacy. I promised an hour to Jesus.

You do not have to give God an hour every day. I encourage most of you not to do that because you will not be able to do that. But everybody can give God at least 10 minutes a day. They have to be quality 10 minutes, not just praying on the way to work. Usually you curse people when you are driving. You are not in deep prayer.

Prayer has to occur in a place where you encounter the Lord. So once you have chosen a time, you have to find a place. The number one place to pray would be in an Adoration Chapel because the God of the Universe is physically present there, but many people do not have that wonderful luxury. I would encourage you to find a place in your home where you can encounter Jesus. It has to be a place set aside. I have a priest classmate who encounters God every day in an easy chair every morning. Next to the chair, he has a candle, which he lights to show the presence of Christ. That is where he says his breviary and drinks his coffee. Every morning he has coffee with Jesus. That works for him.

I also have two great friends who I married a couple of years ago; they are both doctors and they have two children. To make sure that they pray every day, they changed one of their closets into a chapel. It just shows that you can be very busy and married with kids, but you can still find some place in your house to encounter the Risen Lord Jesus!

When you have a place that you walk by during the day, Jesus will call you to sit with Him. If you say you are very busy, He responds, "I know. Come sit with me. I will make it easier for you," even though you might say, "Oh no, I have to get this done." He will keep calling you until you surrender.

Some say I was kind of a strange kid, just like some may say I am a strange adult now. When I was a kid, I had an altar in my room. I had a crucifix there. I had a statue of the Blessed Mother. I had an Infant of Prague statue because it came from my great-great grandmother, and I had a statue of St. Joseph. (Poor St. Joseph was a hollow statue and I hid my cigarettes inside of him. I abused Joseph when I was young. I do not smoke anymore and neither does Joseph.) That was a place where every morning and every night I would go and encounter Jesus. When I walked into the room, it was always a place that Jesus would call me over and I would go over there to meet Him.

Everyone needs a place like that in their home. You do not have to have a full altar. But you could have a chair where you have a crucifix in front of it. Figure out where you can create a place to be alone with the Lord or with the Lord and your family. If you have a place for Him where you encounter Jesus, it just helps tremendously.

As Catholics we use external things to help us experience the Lord. That is why we have smells, bells, and incense. We stand. We kneel. Because when you do those things, you get your whole being involved. Most of my prayer time now is in the main church because I like to be alone. I like to be still and constantly in awe. Every time I am in a church, it is always so inspiring. That is always what the Catholic Church has tried to do. It gives us structures to lift us up, to inspire us, because we are very human people. I need to have a beautiful church around me with all the stars in the sky and all the statues. People may say then that I have weak faith. Okay, then I have weak faith. I still need things to remind me of God's Presence.

The Catholic Church has always been a place where we enter into the presence of the almighty God of heaven. We are taken out of where we normally are, and that is what happens in prayer. God meets us where we are, but takes us where He is. In prayer, God meets us where we are, but He takes us where He is — heaven.

When we encounter God in prayer, we are entering into heaven. Every time you go to Mass you go to heaven. In the book of Revelation, chapter 4, John was in prayer when a door opened, and he could see heaven. So when we are in prayer, we are entering into heaven.

Sometimes in prayer the Lord will not always be gentle with us, and that is okay because he loves us enough to challenge us to the next level. In 1988, I was making a silent retreat before my ordination to the deaconate. My spiritual director was Msgr. James Peterson. He would come in and direct me every day, and he told me to pray and then just open the Word of God and read until the Lord speaks to me. Some people call it "Spiritual Russian Roulette," but it has worked in my life throughout the years. I did not like it though this day because I was ready to take my vow of celibacy and give my life to Jesus Christ. I was 28 years old at the time and I was pretty impressed with myself. "Oh, Lord, look at me. You know I could be doing all these other things, but I am giving you my life. Aren't you excited, Lord?" He was not.

I remember kneeling with my Bible and saying, "Lord, speak to my heart your word." I opened up my Bible and it came to John 5:42 and it read: *It is simply that I know you, and you do not have the love of God in your hearts.*

Bang! I closed that book and thought, "I can't believe you said that to me. Are you out of your mind? I am a virgin, Lord. How many of your people are still virgins? I am giving you my life. I am taking a vow of celibacy and you say 'I have no love of you.'" So I closed the Bible, left my prayer time and went to take a nap. (Because that is how you ignore God — you take a nap.) When I went for my next prayer period, I said, "Okay, Lord, speak to my heart with your word. Come Holy Spirit." And I opened up the Bible again and it opened to John 5:42 a second time. It said, *It is simply that I know you, and you do not have the love of God in your hearts.*

I closed the book and yelled at God. "I don't know what else I can do for you. What else do you want from me, God? I am giving you my life. I am going to be a priest." I came back after I got all that out of my system for my third prayer hour. I knelt before the Lord and said, "Jesus, speak to my heart your word, but be nice to me, would you." I opened up the Word of God, and, once again, the same verse — John 5:42: *It is simply that I know you, and you do not have the love of God in your hearts.* I started to cry. I closed the Bible and just looked at Jesus in the Blessed Sacrament, and I said, "You are right. I only love myself. I am doing all this for me. Jesus, you who are God, you who created me, re-create me and put love of you in my heart."

The Lord was saying very clearly and honestly to me that I was in love with myself more than Him. But He can change that! When you and I acknowledge that we do not love Him enough, then we can look to Jesus and give Him permission to change our hearts. The great thing is that He did it for me. I do love God more than anything else, not perfectly, but I do. Can I love Him more? Oh yeah. Do I want to love Him more? Oh yeah.

In order to grow, we have to allow the Lord to reveal ourselves to ourselves, where we are, who we are. Sometimes He will kick you in the butt. Sometimes He will say things to you that will make you think He is being mean or unkind. He was not being mean to me that day. He was preparing me to enter into a deeper relationship. He had to reveal myself to me as I am before I could go on to fall in love with Him. I had to repent of loving myself.

When you encounter the living God, it is not always going to be gentle, but it is always going to be loving. Sometimes it will include suffering. When that happens, give it to God and

He will say that He is with you in the midst of this just like He was with Jesus on the cross. You will never be alone.

In fast summary then, the first thing you need to do is to give time to God every day. Next you find a place to pray. After you find a place, now you have to surrender. I want to give you a way to help you to surrender and know that you are loved by God.

This is the prayer formula that I have led people with in the last twenty years or so, and it is a pattern that I use and have found very helpful in creating an encounter with Jesus, and can bear much fruit.

Take five minutes every day. Go to your place where you meet God. Be still and center on the reality that God is present with you. Now do the following three things:

1. Tell God, "I am sorry." Go through your sins and repent of them. Invite Jesus to be your Savior.
2. Tell God, "I surrender." Surrender your heart to Jesus and invite Him to take control of your life. Allow Jesus to be your Lord.
3. Ask God, "Hold me." Ask Jesus to hold you, and be still and listen to Him. Just let Him love you.

Now this will take you about five minutes at first. One minute on "I am sorry." One minute on "I surrender." Three minutes on "Hold me." Notice the most amount of time is spent on "Hold me," allowing God to have full control, listening to Him, and letting Him love you. The way you end this prayer experience is to pray with Jesus the prayer that He taught us — the Our Father.[4]

If you do this every day, you will begin to see a change in your life — I promise. But the question is will you do it?

Let us explore this in greater detail.

First, say, "I am sorry." The first thing Jesus commanded us was, "Repent." Sin can keep us from God. So after saying you are sorry, go through your sins with the Lord. No excuses. Just tell Him you are sorry. He was there when you committed every sin and yet He never stopped loving you. He was right there and you hurt Him, but the only thing He wants to do is to forgive you. That forgiveness happens when you repent and tell Him you are sorry for all your sins. As you tell Jesus you are sorry, imagine He takes His hand, and places it over your head and one drop of the blood that was shed at Calvary now covers your whole being as He says, "I forgive you." He died on the cross to forgive you. He wants to forgive you. He longs to forgive you. Just let Him.

The next thing that needs to happen in daily prayer is the "I surrender" part. Imagine that you have your hands cupped in front as if you are trying to hold water in them. I want you to think of those sins that you just gave to Jesus and place those and all the sins of your past in your life in your hands. Then think about your happiest moments in life. When you were with someone you love. When one of your children was born. Think about those happy times. Place those now in your hands. Think about the saddest times in your life when someone you loved died or someone hurt you or a time of great suffering. Place all that now in your hands. Take your whole past, the good, the bad, the sorrow, the joy, the sin, the holiness, put it all in your hands. You can't do anything about the past, so spiritually place it in your hands. Take this moment, the only moment you have, and spiritually place that in your hands. Take the future, whatever time you have left on this earth, and spiritually place that in your hands.

Now surrender it all to Jesus. Say, "Jesus, all that I am, just as I am, my past, my present, my future, I surrender it all to you." Give it all to the Lord and look at Him as you give Him your life. Look at the smile on His face. He has waited all of eternity for you to surrender everything to Him. He loves you more than you will ever love yourself. He wants you to be happy more than you want to be happy. He looks at you and says, "I will never let you go."

Now comes the most important part of the prayer. This is the one most people struggle with the most. The God of the Universe wants to embrace you, so you have to become a little boy or a little girl no matter how old you are now. You look at the God of the Universe, and you say "Jesus, hold me." Feel Christ, the God of the Universe, put His arms around you. Take your head and place it on His chest as John the Evangelist did at the Last Supper. Listen to His heartbeat. Every time His heart beats, He says, "I love you. I love you. I love you." Don't say a word. Be still and know that He is God. Be still and let God love you for the next few moments.

Now, as you are in the arms of Jesus, He says to you, "I want you to know that your Father, my Father, is who I came to reveal to you." And so He looks at you and says. "Pray with me in the words that I taught you." Now in silence, slowly in your heart with Jesus in your arms, pray with Him the words He taught you:

> Our Father, who art in heaven,
> hallowed be thy name;
> thy kingdom come;
> thy will be done
> on earth as it is in heaven.
> Give us this day our daily bread;
> and forgive us our trespasses
> as we forgive those
> who trespass against us;
> and lead us not into temptation,
> but deliver us from evil.
> Amen.

There is never a moment in your whole life where you are alone — never. Jesus Christ is always with you. More than that, when Jesus embraces you, He pulls you into himself, and you become one with him. You and Jesus become one when you pray. That's the point. What you have to do is enter into this relationship. Be still with Him. Pray with Him. Allow the God of the Universe to embrace you. Do it every day.

Five minutes a day will change your life. Five minutes a day in the arms of your Father, the arms of Jesus, the power of the Spirit will change everything about you. It is a process, but when you come to know that you are loved you have nothing to be afraid of.

STEPS TO SURRENDERING YOUR LIFE

1. Commit to daily time with God.
2. Create a place in your home to encounter God every day.
3. In your daily encounter with God say:

   (1) I am sorry.
   (2) I surrender.
   (3) Hold me.

   End by saying the "Our Father" with Jesus.

A PRAYER TO HELP YOU ON YOUR WAY

Prayer of Abandonment

Father,
I abandon myself into your hands; do with me what you will.
Whatever you may do, I thank you:

SURRENDER!

I am ready for all, I accept all.
Let only your will be done in me, and in all your creatures.
I wish no more than this, O Lord.

Into your hands I commend my soul;
I offer it to you
with all the love of my heart,
for I love you, Lord,
and so need to give myself to you,
to surrender myself into your hands,
without reserve,
and with boundless confidence,
for you are my Father.
Amen.

— VEN. CHARLES DE FOUCAULD

CHAPTER 6

Surrender and Discover God's Will!

"A voice shall sound in your ears: 'This is the way; walk in it.'" (Isaiah 30:21, NAB)

God has a specific plan for your life! He created you for a specific purpose. Your job is to figure out what it is. Isaiah tells us, *A voice shall sound in your ears: This is the way; walk in it.* But the question is how do you hear His voice and discover His will?

If you are reading this chapter before you've read the first part of the book, STOP! Read the first five chapters before you get to this chapter. You cannot take the steps that I am going to give you without doing everything that comes before them first. This isn't about getting a "sign" and having everything fall into place. It's about being in a relationship with Jesus Christ and listening and hearing His voice as He speaks to you. It is very important that you are in this relationship, that you are a disciple, before you can discover God's will for your life.

The first thing that you have to realize when you are trying to discern the will of God is that God has a plan for your life. Most people think that God just sits back and says, "Okay, go for it," because He gave us free will and we can do anything we want. Well, you can do anything you want and He did give you free will, but He has a plan for your life. You can do what you want or what He wants — it is your choice.

Before you were ever born, God had a specific will for your life. We see in the call of Jeremiah, *Before I formed you in the womb I knew you. Before you were born I dedicated you a prophet to the nations I appointed you* (see Jeremiah 1:5). Just as God had had a plan for Jeremiah, He has one for you!

We see this also in Mary, God's Mother. The Church teaches that from the moment she was conceived in the womb of her mother Anne, Mary was preserved from original sin. We call this doctrine "The Immaculate Conception." She was preserved from sin because Jesus would receive His humanity from her, and since He could not take on anything sinful, God put the grace of Jesus' death on her at the moment she was conceived. And because God lives in an "Eternal Now" with no past or future, He could do this for Mary at her conception. Before God even formed her in the womb of her mother, God had a plan for Mary. Now Mary did not have to cooperate with that plan. She could have said no. If she didn't have a choice to say "yes" or "no," then she would have been no better than my dog. She would not have any free will. She had to choose to cooperate with God's plan for her, which she did whole-heartedly when she cried out "*Fiat*" — let it be done to me. The point is that God had a plan for her and He has a plan for you!

When we look at Jesus Christ, He, too, had a purpose that He was sent to earth to fulfill. Jesus knew that purpose and lived for that. He often spoke about His "Hour." For instance saying, *My hour has not yet come* (see John 2:4; John 7:30; John 8:20; John 12:23). The hour for Jesus was the moment He was to die on the cross. That is what He was begotten for, that was His vocation from God His Father.

One year at the celebration of the Lord's Passion on Good Friday, I was on the altar with a priest, who is no longer a priest. He was preaching the homily and said that it was not God's will for Jesus to die on the cross. I almost strangled him. I was speechless. He was saying that God loves us but He really did not want His Son to do die for us. Excuse me! The whole reason that Christ was born was to fulfill the will of His Father, and His Father's will was that He was to die for our sins. Period!

God has a plan for every one of you. As long as you are alive, God still has a plan for you. Every day when you wake up, God has a plan for your day. This is why discernment is so important. You have a vocation, a reason that God created you, but every day God has a plan for your life. When we have a listening heart, we follow that plan.

When people come to me and ask, "What does God want? Where should I go? What should I do with my life?" I tell them that know your life is already planned by God. What you need to discover is what He wants you to do, but you don't need to make it up as you go.

Let me give you an example from my life. From all eternity, God created me to be a priest. You can tell because it clicks in my life. This is what I do even though I was thrown out of seminary by the vocation director, who said, "Larry, we are throwing you out because it is like this. It is your personality. It is like you have a cancer. You would never be a good priest." Well, thank you Father for sharing that with me. But God knew, and I knew, that God had a plan for me. I never separated myself from that.

When I was 17, I was praying in the Church of the Epiphany in Pittsburgh, Pennsylvania. I knelt before the God of the Universe in the Eucharist and asked, "Jesus, what do you want me to do?" He told me to be a priest. It didn't happen the first time. I had to ask for six, seven eight months. I knelt there every day asking, "God what do you want me to do? I will do anything that you want. God tell me what to do. I will do anything you want."

Now at that time my life was going in an altogether different direction. I had a girlfriend. I wanted to do things "my way." I wanted to be married. I wanted to have children. I was going to be a draftsman. I was going to do all of these things. I was a pagan in lots of ways, but when I knelt before the Lord I gave Him permission. "Whatever you want Lord. I know you have a plan for my life."

Then one day He told me that He wanted me to be a priest. Now at that time everybody was against the idea. My pastor would not recommend me to go to seminary. I went to him and said, "You at least have to give me my baptismal certificate." He gave it to me and said, "Good luck on your fantasy."

My family was not very supportive at first. My dad was not Catholic and he thought that I was wasting my talents being a priest. He always thought I should be a lawyer! He used to write me letters when I was in seminary telling me that I was destined for better things than being a priest.

My mother did not really care one way or the other. She did not go to Church at the time and really thought that the Church just kept people from God with all its rules. You know, like, "You cannot go to Communion if you are in a bad marriage," etc.

I often used to wonder where I came from — my life views were so different from my family's.

My grandmother was supportive of me, but she always thought it was a phase. She thought that later on I would come back and get married.

I also had a girlfriend I had to leave when I entered the seminary. She also just thought it was a phase I was going through. She would write me letters when I was in the seminary. I still have all of my letters from seminary. Maybe someday someone will find them and think what is this because all of her letters to me are addressed to "Larry 'Hot lips' Richards." Remember, I was a very typical high school kid, not the one you would think would go to seminary. However, the Lord entered my life, changed me, and set me in an altogether different direction for my life.

From the very beginning of my creation, God had a plan for me just as God has a plan for you. You have to believe that. You have to believe that your life is not a bunch of chaos that you try to make the best of with what you have been dealt. Your life is a product of the plan of God, but for it to make sense, you have to say "yes" to His plan. Just like Jeremiah, just like Mary, just like Jesus.

In Ephesians 1:4, St. Paul reminds us, *God chose us in Him before the world began.* We have already talked about this when we discussed God's general will for everyone, but it also means that He has a plan for you that was in place before the world began. You are not a mistake; you were planned. He has chosen you by name. Now you must cooperate with this plan and believe in this reality. This is the first step in discovering God's will for your life.

The second step requires that you have faith in His plan. This means that you trust that His plan is better than your plan. You might have a plan for your life but God has a plan, too. All too often, the plans are different.

I believe most people want only their will, not God's will. You can tell when they are living their will because they do not have peace. They are always trying the next thing. They are always trying to fill up the emptiness because they are not doing what they were created to do. Now God can fix that, if you let Him and do it His way.

This has to be practical. For instance, when people come to me asking about marriage, I tell them, "You don't get married until God tells you this is the one to marry." Do not marry someone just because you think this is a nice person. Ask instead, "Can I share my soul with this person?" Do not just find anybody to get along with now. Find the one God created for you.

God knows who you are going to marry. He created someone just for you, but He will let you marry anybody you want.

I once heard a story that Ruth Graham, the wife of Billy Graham, used to tell. "I am so glad God says 'no' to prayer. Otherwise I would have married the wrong person three different times." What she meant was that she dated three different men and she said to God, "Oh, this is the one that I want. This is the one I want to marry." God said, "No." She dated another person and again God said, "No." She found a third person and again God said, "No." Finally, He gave her Billy Graham and God said, "Yes!" She had waited until God said, "Yes." That is what we must do in our own lives. God's will is always better than your will. You cannot see tomorrow, but He can. He wants you to be happy more than you want to be happy.

Because of the free will He gives us, we can really mess up, but that is not what God wants. That is why it is very important before you and I do anything, we discern it. We take time and ask, "God is this what you want of me?" Then if it comes down to choosing God's will or my will, we choose to do God's will. Always. Once you believe that God has a plan, you have got to be willing to discard your plan for His plan. That is going to take some faith. It is not easy. I know. Who said it would be?

I have a process that has worked for me both in my own life and in helping people discern God's will for their lives. Now different people have different methods and there is not any single best way to do it, but every way has to have specific things in place. Then, once you do them, you must have patience.

In Hebrews 10:35–36, we read, *Do not, then, surrender your confidence: it will have great reward.* You need patience to do God's will and receive what He has promised. We need patience. (I don't do that very well. As anyone can tell, I don't have patience.) Embrace the will of God by making an act of faith and then have patience.

When I tell people how to discern God's will, I tell them they cannot just go into the chapel for five minutes and expect God to tell them what to do. It might take a week. It might take a month. It might take six months. It might take a year. God does not give you the ticket to get on the train until the train comes into the station. That can be scary because we want to know our future. God never tells us our future. That is just the way it is. As I write this book, I have the coming year all planned out. Now do you think that this year is going to work the way I have planned it? Absolutely not! Every time I plan a week ahead of time it gets changed. We can put this nice plan together, but then we have to say, "Okay, God, if you will it." As James 4:15 tells us, *If God wills it we will do this or that.* Don't be presumptuous that something is going to happen. You have to say if God wills this, then it will be. I have to want what God wants because He might change my plan. We must be open to whatever He is calling us to. His plan is better than my plan even when I have my plan planned. In the morning, I might have a great plan for the day, but almost never does the day go the way I want it to go. When things happen, you and I have to say, "Your will be done. Okay, you took me a way that I didn't want to go, but your will be done." You can make plans, but make sure your plans are tentative based on God's will.

The next step in discerning God's will is to deal with the obstacles in our life. One of these is our past. Too many people let their past dictate their future. Now let me be very clear here in order to make sure you get this into your being. The devil always keeps us focused on ourselves and our past, be it good or bad. God always keeps us focused on Him and the future.

The greatest example of this is St. Peter walking on the water (see Matthew 14:22–33). As long as Peter was looking at Jesus, he was fine. He could walk on water because that was God's will for him. As long as Peter was looking at Jesus, he was fine. The same is true for you — as long as you are looking at God and His will and not yourself and your weakness or the storm around you, you will be fine. As soon as Peter started looking at himself or at the situation, he began to fall. How did he get back up? He focused on Jesus. He cried out, *Lord, save me!* So it is in our own lives. We focus on what Christ is calling us to do. We focus on the future and we let the past be past. It doesn't matter where you have been. It only matters where you are going.

As we have already seen in Chapter 3, another obstacle to discerning God's will is our sin. Sin keeps you from doing God's will because you are doing your own will. You have to deal with your sin, which means you repent and surrender to God and start being obedient to Him and His law.

One of the biggest obstacles is fear. What did Jesus say about fear? *Fear is useless, what is needed is trust* (see Mark 5:36). If God says fear is useless, then it is useless. So why do we let our fears determine what our vocation will be? God loves you. He knows how it is going to work out in the end. You need to look at it this way: since God is in the eternal now, you are already in heaven or hell before Him. He already knows how it is going to work out. He knows tomorrow. He can see it. He has already been there. He says, "I am here. Do not worry. Come here. I am going to take care of you." But so often we say, "Well, I don't know about that, God."

You cannot let fear enter into any of your discernment. Fear is the enemy of discernment. Fear can do nothing to help you with your discernment. Fear always comes from the devil. It never comes from God. Jesus said, *Fear is useless*, and then He added, *What is needed is trust* (see Mark 5:36). What helps us to trust? Love. 1 John 4:18 says, *Perfect love casts out all fear.* When we are in love with God, we can trust Him, because we know Him. Think about the nicest, kindest person you know; God is one thousand times more caring! The more you come to know how much He loves you, the more you will know that He will take care of you.

Now some people like to argue with me by saying that we need to be afraid of God. They quote the Scriptures that read, *Fear of the Lord is the beginning of wisdom* (see Proverbs 1:7). They also like to point out that "fear of the Lord" is one of the seven gifts of the Holy Spirit. But this is not the type of fear that we are talking about here. We are talking about the kind of fear that is only concerned about self and what is going to happen to me, not fear that has to do with the Lord. That is a different fear. That is the awe and amazement we feel when we realize who God is. The kind of fear that comes from the devil is an obstacle of our will. It is a wanting to do things our way instead of God's way.

When you are worried or afraid, combat it with trust. The best way to do this when you are tempted to be afraid is cry out to Jesus a hundred times a day: "Jesus, I trust in you!" When Jesus appeared to St. Faustina, giving her the message of Divine Mercy, He told her that He wants people to trust. He asked her to have an image of Him painted and under the image have written, "Jesus, I trust in you." If you struggle with fear, then I encourage you to get one of those pictures, put it in your prayer place and tell Jesus often that you trust Him. It will drive the devil crazy!

The next thing that helps us to discern, and this is key, is the Holy Spirit. One of the gifts of the Holy Spirit is discernment of spirits. 1 Corinthians 12:10 states, *To one He gives discernment or distinguishing of spirits.* It is the Holy Spirit who reveals to us the mind of God and leads us in His holy will. We see this in the life of Jesus right from the beginning of His ministry. In Luke 4:1, after Jesus is baptized, it states, *Jesus, full of the Holy Spirit, then returned from the Jordan and was conducted by the Spirit into the desert.* Another word for "conducted" is "led," so if Jesus who is God needed the Holy Spirit in His humanity, and He lets the Holy Spirit lead Him, so it must be in our lives!

That is why discerning God's will is not magic. It is not superstition. It is not asking for a sign from heaven. That is not being led by the Holy Spirit. That is being led by a sign. Jesus does not just live in the Holy Spirit. He gives the Holy Spirit to us to lead us. In John 14:26, we read, *The Paraclete, the Holy Spirit whom the Father will send in my name will instruct you in everything and remind you of all that I told you.* Then in John 16:13, He says, *When the Spirit, when He comes however being the Spirit of Truth He will guide you to all truth. He will not speak of His own, He will only speak what He hears and will announce to you the things that are to come.* As I have said before, one of the greatest practices to help you in this is the daily prayer to the Holy Spirit, in which you give the Spirit of God permission to lead you.

The Acts of the Apostles are filled with accounts of how the Holy Spirit would compel people in the early Church. In Acts 8:29, it reads, *The Spirit said to Philip, "Go and catch up with that carriage" and Philip ran ahead and he had did as the Spirit had said.* Then in Acts 13:1–3, we read, *There was in the Church of Antioch certain prophets and teachers. On one occasion while they were engaged in the Liturgy of the Lord and they were fasting, the Holy Spirit spoke to them.* This is interesting because they were fasting in the middle of Mass, and Mass is one of the things that helps you in discernment. One of the ways that you and I can be open to discernment is to fast and go to daily Mass and then the Spirit can speak to you. Fasting opens you up to receive His will. When you are fasting at Mass, you become an open vessel to be filled with God.

One other thing that you must do is discern whether it is the Holy Spirit or whether it is an evil spirit. The evil spirit can come to us and appear as something good. The devil often appears as an angel of light, appearing to be good. The devil can appear in all kinds of ways. The demon once appeared to St. Padre Pio as the Blessed Mother and once as Jesus. St. Pio sprinkled holy water and said, "Praised be Jesus Christ," and the devil left. 1 John 4:1–6 tells us that we need to test the spirits. The way we do that is through the power of the Holy Spirit. One of the ways you test if something is from the Holy Spirit or not is that the Holy Spirit would not go against Scripture or against the teaching of the Church. And the Holy Spirit is always going to be for the building up of the community, not the building up of the self. A question to ask is, "Is it for the good of all or the good of just me?" There are no Lone Rangers in Christianity. It is always about the whole community and how I grow and build up the community of Christ.

Another gift that we are given to help us discern the Holy Spirit is angels. The main purpose of an angel is to convey the will of God to us. When you read Tobit in the Old Testament, Raphael, the Archangel, appears in Tobit 5:4 to lead Tobias through all of these different things. He appears and says, *I am Raphael, one of the seven angels that stands before the face of God.* Another example is the Blessed Mother in Luke 1:26–38 where the angel Gabriel appears and reveals the will of God to her. And an angel appears in a dream to Joseph in Matthew 1:20. So the angels convey God's will to us.

Padre Pio was very big about praying to your guardian angel every day. Once when the devils were attacking him, his guardian angel was singing and dancing around his head. Padre Pio could see his guardian angel. He cried out to his angel, "You help me! You help me!" But the demons kept beating the heck out Padre Pio. Finally, the angel got rid of all the demons beating him up. Then Padre Pio yelled at his angel and the angel felt very bad.

You also have an angel given to you by God Himself to guard you and lead you. Remember the prayer of the guardian angel?

"O angel of God my guardian dear, by whom God's love, entrust thee here. Ever this day be at my side, to light and guard, to lead and guide. Amen." In that prayer, you are asking the angel of God to lead you. You were given your Guardian angel when you were born to get you to heaven. So if you have a discerning heart and you pray to your guardian angel, you have somebody that is always with you that is going to help you.

Padre Pio would encourage people to pray to their guardian angels for protection. When I was a kid I had an interesting experience. I was four or five years old and was at my grandmother's house in Pittsburgh. In those days, we all had porches or steps in the front of the house. We always sat out in front and talked to one another. Everybody knew one another. In our neighborhood, we parked on both sides of the street. My grandmother's house was one of the few that had a big tree in front of it.

One day when I was out playing, I was told not to leave the curb. And what do kids do? They leave the curb. I was running across the street just as a car was coming up. It almost hit me, but I felt someone behind me actually pull me away from that car. My grandmother started screaming. I turned around and asked, "Who grabbed me?" Nobody had grabbed me. I will never forget my grandmother saying, "It was your angel." It was a physical manifestation of an angel for me because I felt it. I will never forget it.

Another time I was driving on a back road at night. As I was driving, my safety belt grabbed me and started pulling me back. So I slowed down and as I did, a big deer ran in front of the car. I could have hit and killed the deer and I might have been killed, but because my seat belt was being pulled back, I slowed down. My guardian angel sure got my attention!

Your angel has been given to you by God to lead you in the will of God. Angels are real and we all have these angels to lead us and guide us. To get their help, say a daily prayer to your guardian angel.

Now you must remember that every step you take, every decision, is either a step toward God and His will or away from God and His will. There are no neutral steps. You are either walking toward God or you are walking away from God. How do we make this practical? How to you make a daily decision? How do you decide if God wants you to be a priest? If God wants you to be a nun? If God wants you to marry, or what college to go to or which job to take? How do I decide this practically?

Let me give you this answer. Let's say you have five options in front of you. There is no sin in any of these options. They are all good choices. In prayer put all of your options down on separate pieces of paper. Five options, five sheets of paper.

Again in prayer go through the good and the bad of each of these with God. What are the pros? What are the cons? Will this make me more loving of God and others? That is the number one question that all of your choices have to answer.

Now this is going to take time and this is a process, so be patient. You don't do this once. You do it many times, over many days. You take each of these pieces of paper individually and you pray with them. "Is this what You want me to do God?"

Of course before you do this you have to give God permission to have His will done in your life. You say to Him, "I will only do what you want." If you are making any decision in your life, if it is going to be a life-changing decision, you have to make sure that you are praying about it and that you tell God that you only want what He wants.

Then you take each option separately in your days of prayer, and you ask, "Is this what you want? If I were to die today and I did this, is this what you want me to do?" Some things God will give you no peace about, so you get rid of those options right away. By "peace" I mean "oneness with God, oneness with others, oneness with yourself." It is a tranquillity of oneness — it clicks. It is like putting the last piece of a puzzle in place. The reason it "clicks" is because this is what you were created for.

By definition as a Christian we should have peace. When we lose peace, we know that we are not in the will of God. So if one choice brings anxiety or confusion, that is never of God. Get rid of it. *God is a God, not of confusion, but of peace* (see 1 Corinthians 14:33).

Now you pray for a couple more days and by now you may have discarded three of the five. You keep praying with the remaining two pieces of paper, those two choices, until God makes it clear to you what He wants you to do, remembering that "in His will is our peace" (Dante's *Paradiso*, Canticle 3, verse 85). By definition if I lose my peace there is something wrong in my life. You have to look at two things you lose your peace. One, you are not doing the will of God. All of the red flags should go up. Or two, you are in sin which is really the same thing. It's easy to figure out which it is. If you go to confession and rid yourself of the serious sin and still don't have peace, it's because you are not doing what God wants you to do.

Another piece of advice to help you best discern God's will is to get a spiritual director. St. Philip Neri said, "Those who have themselves for a spiritual director have a fool for a spiritual director." A spiritual director is the best way to come to know the will of God. As St. Teresa of Ávila said, "To obey your director is to obey God."

The reason that this is so important is because I sometimes think I know what God wants and I am totally wrong. Years ago, after the first Gulf War broke out, I felt that God was calling me to be a Navy chaplain. So I called the bishop and asked permission and he said, "Okay, Larry, I will let you go." I was all excited. Then as an afterthought, I realized that I had not talked to my spiritual director about this, so I went and told my spiritual director. He looked at me and said, "Absolutely not!" I said, "What? I already asked the bishop and he said okay."

"Absolutely not!" he said to me.

I said, "What am I supposed to do?"

He said, "You call the bishop, and you tell him your spiritual director said 'no.'" So I called up the bishop and told him and he just said, "Okay, Larry." I was not a happy person at first, but God had a better plan, and He told me that through my spiritual director.

If I had gone into the Navy, I would have had an altogether different life. I would probably never be doing what I am doing right now. I would have never started The Reason for Our Hope Foundation. I would never have given talks. I would never have been serving at a wonderful parish. To obey my director was to obey God.

Now, before you pick a director, make sure your director knows God. You need to be very careful when you are doing this! What you must do is find someone who knows Jesus better than you. Then you put yourself under him or her as your spiritual director.

Sometimes people think they will just get a priest because all priests know God. Not true. Priests do not automatically know God.

If you are going to see a priest, watch the way he says Mass. If he is in love with Jesus in the Eucharist and the people can see that he loves Jesus, he is a good one to choose. You can tell when a person loves Jesus and when they are going through the motions.

You can also find that love in a religious sister or a holy layperson. I usually encourage women to see women and men to see men, because we have different spirits. But this is not a hard rule. I once had a religious sister as my spiritual director when I was in the major seminary, and she was very helpful in my walk with Christ. So just make sure you pray about the person you are going to choose before you make your choice.

You might want to have a few sessions with your potential spiritual director before you make it official. If that person brings you peace and yet challenges you to grow in your love of God and others, then stay with him or her. Once you put yourself under the direction of a director, remember that "to obey your director is to obey God." Your spiritual director will clearly show God's will for you. That is why you have to make sure your director knows the God of the Universe.

You can also ask people you know who are spiritual to help you discern God's will. Spiritual means that they are praying and loving. But they must also be disinterested in your decision. For instance, you don't ask your mother what college you should go to because your mother is going to want you to be close to her or she is going to want you to be far away from her. So she will make suggestions based on the way she feels, not necessarily on God's will for you.

When I am a spiritual director to men in seminary, my job is to not keep them there. My job is to lead them in God's will for them. I tell them: "You have to discern God's will. Do not try to make me happy. Do not try to make your parents happy. You have got to make God happy." Do not ever do anything to just make someone else happy when it comes to discernment of God's will. You have to make God happy. You have to do God's will, so bounce it off someone who is a neutral party in your decision.

I work things out by talking with people, so when I am making a decision I pray about it, I talk to my spiritual director, but I also talk to spiritual people. Why is this important? Because we are one body in the Body of Christ, so each of us can give a different insight into the body and help us in our struggles with discernment.

As I was talking to another priest about this he said, "Just tell them to have common sense." Well, sometimes God does not work through common sense. God told an old man named Abram to leave everything and go where God would show him (see Genesis 12:1). He tells a 14-year-old woman she is going to be the Mother of God and she is not going to have sex to do it (see Luke 1:26–38) — that is not common sense! So common sense isn't always the way of discerning God's will.

A final thought that will help you in your discernment process. A great spiritual principle for you to know is: "God does not send a person to China without first putting the love of China in their heart." Once I had one of my spiritual directees who was discerning priesthood call me and start to cry. "Father, if God wants me to be a priest, I'll be a priest, but I really love this girl." I told him, "Son, that is a pretty good sign that God does not want you to be a priest!" You will always find joy in His will — even if it kills you. God will prepare you. You might not be all excited about it at first, but if it is of God, He will change your heart toward what He wants you to do.

You will know God's will when you discern what gives you peace. You will know it. Once you know God's will, then you are going to have to live it, and that means you become a living sacrifice, which is what the next chapter is about.

STEPS TO SURRENDERING YOUR LIFE

1. Believe that God has a specific plan for your life.
2. Believe His plan is better than yours.
3. Be Patient.
4. Ask God to remove all fear.
5. Surrender your will to His.
6. Ask the Holy Spirit for help.
7. Write down your options.

8. Focus on what gives you peace.
9. Get input from others or a spiritual director.
10. Do whatever gives you God's peace.

A Prayer to Help You on Your Way

Prayer to the Holy Spirit

Oh, Holy Spirit, beloved of my soul, I adore you.
Enlighten me, guide me, strengthen me, console me.
Tell me what I should do; give me your orders.
I promise to submit myself to all that you desire of me
and to accept all that you permit to happen to me.
Let me only know your will.

— Joseph Cardinal Mercier

CHAPTER 7

Surrender and Live God's Will!

"I urge you therefore, brothers, by the mercies of God, to offer your bodies as a living sacrifice, holy and pleasing to God, your spiritual worship." (Romans 12:1, NAB)

There is an interesting story attributed to St. Francis. One day he was hoeing his garden. Someone came up to him and asked, "Francis, what if I were to tell you that in three hours you would be dead. What would you do?" St. Francis said, "I would keep hoeing my garden." He was able to say that because he was doing the will of God. The key to this kind of peace is to live every day so that no matter what happens, if God calls you home today, it does not matter. You keep doing what you are doing because this is God's will.

The way we do this, as we have been talking throughout the whole book, is to decide to live God's way, not our way. St. Paul instructs us how to do this in Romans 12:1: *And now my brothers I beg you through the mercy of God to offer your bodies as a living sacrifice. Holy and acceptable to God, your spiritual worship. Do not conform yourselves to this age but be transformed by the renewal of your mind so that you may judge what is God's will what is good, what is pleasing, what is perfect.*

What is a living sacrifice? Do you ever think about what that means to be a living sacrifice? A sacrifice means you give your life away. Living means you are still alive while you do it. So being a living sacrifice means it is going to hurt. (Don't you hate that? I hate that.)

Remember in Chapter 4 I told you about the priest who, when I was complaining about all the things I had to do, told me how great it was that our weariness refreshes others? That hit me right between the eyes! I have been ordained many years and I never heard that. He was so right. When you and I become a living sacrifice and we are tired, we are giving others refreshment. That is what it is to be a living sacrifice. You and I are not being a sacrifice for no reason. We do it to give life to others. What a great and glorious thing that our tiredness is refreshing to others.

For you and I to be a living sacrifice means to live as the crucified One. Christ is inside of us. When people see us, they should be seeing the icon of the Crucified. This means that my life is for others. Jesus gave His life for you and now you must do the same. We must say, "God, I want you to use me today, not so I can get what I want done but so that I can do what you want." That is an exciting thing.

Every day when I wake up I try to do this, but I usually take it back five minutes after I give it to Him! However, I always try to say, "God I want what you want today. I fall on my knees and say, "Jesus, I love you and give you my life. Let your will be done. Use me, Lord, for Your glory." There are some days when I am excited, and I think, "What is going to happen today?" And other days I really don't want to know, because I'm dreading it and I think, "Oh I wonder what is going to happen today? UGH!"

The way I can tell the difference is when I am focusing on me if I have the "UGH!" feeling. When I am focusing on God, I feel excited. But that doesn't mean there won't be a cost. When I am speaking at a men's conference or a parish mission, I wake up thinking, "People's lives are going to change today," but I also know that it is going to cost me. It is going to cost me my life, but people's lives are going to change. So there is the excitement. When I wake up and I am in Christ, then there is excitement. When I wake up and I am in me, then there is dread.

We become saints when our will and God's will become one. This is where St. Francis was when he said he would continue doing what he was doing even if he were to die within the hour, and this is where we need to be, too. To establish that, we need to be at peace. When we lose peace, we know that something is wrong. As we talked about before, that means either we are in mortal sin and we need to repent or we are not doing God's will.

Day in and day out, we need to be in the will of God, to be in peace. Now if we are at peace, one of the biggest things we have to do is live Matthew 6:33: *Seek ye first the kingdom of heaven and then everything else will be given to you.*

The problem with most people is that they seek everything else and hope to get the kingdom. We need to be seeking the kingdom of God first. And the Kingdom of Heaven is simply the will of God on earth. When we start living God's will, we start experiencing heaven on earth. St. Catherine of Siena said, "All the way to heaven is heaven because Jesus said, 'I am the way.'" So when we start living God's will, we get a foretaste of heaven. This is reflected in the Lord's Prayer when we say, "Thy kingdom come, thy will be done on earth as it is in heaven." When I am doing God's will on earth, I am experiencing heaven. I am getting a glimpse of it in my daily life because when I am doing God's will I am living, if you will, in heaven. I am in union with God. God and I have become one in His will.

Let's look at John 15. I love the Fifteenth Chapter of John's Gospel! If anyone ever asks me where they should begin reading the Bible, I always say John 15 because it teaches us so much. It begins with, *I am the vine, you are the branches.* Then it goes on to say, *Live on in me as I do in you* (see John 15:4). Think about it. He lives in us and we live in Him. He is Emmanuel, "God with us."

The question is not whether God is always with us; of course He is always with us. He lives in us — by definition. The question is, "Do we live in Him?" We need to ask, "Do I dwell with Him? Am I with God? Am I walking in His will? Am I living in the very person of Jesus Christ?" When He states, *I am the vine, you are the branches,* He goes on to say, *Apart from me you can do nothing* (see John 15:5).

It's really very simple. Am I building up the kingdom of heaven or am I building up my own kingdom? Am I putting God's name first and proclaiming His name, or am I proclaiming my name? Am I doing everything for God's glory, or for my glory? We have to focus on this every day. If I am going to live God's will, it has to be because I first seek the kingdom. Then He promises everything else will fall into place.

The core of the chapter is John 15:9, *As the Father has loved me, so I love you.* If you and I really meditated on that verse every day, our lives would be transformed. Just as much as God the Father loves Jesus, that is how much He loves us. One might even argue that God loves us more than Jesus because He let Jesus die for us. That is unbelievable. The God of the Universe looked at you, He looked at Jesus, and He chose you. He let Jesus Christ die for your sins because He loved you. He was willing to give up everything for love of you and me.

After Jesus tells us that we are loved, He commands us to live in His love. This is the key to living in peace and walking in God's will — living in His love! Thus, living the will of God is living in such a way that you know you are loved and that you dwell in His love. Live this way and know His peace.

How do we live in His love? Jesus tells us, *You will live in my love if you keep my commandments even as I have kept my Father's commandments* (see John 15:10). Jesus is saying that the way I live in my Father's love, the way I have peace, is to obey Him. I obey Him in the way I live my life. So if we want to have the same peace as Christ did, if we want to live in His love every day, we have to keep His commandments.

When we talk about keeping commandments, most people talk about the Ten Commandments, but those are not the commandments of Jesus. In John 15:12, He says, *This is my commandment; love one another as I have loved you.* Of course we are to keep the Ten Commandments, but we need to go way beyond them and live the commandment of love.

In John 15:11, He says, *All this I have told you so that my joy may be in you and your joy may be complete.* This is how we are supposed to live every day and how we are supposed to live the will of God. When we are living in the commandment of God, when we are living in His will, when we are living in His love, we will have joy.

In Chapter 2, I related to you a story about being in Rome with the Missionaries of Charity years ago, and I want to now share with you a little more about my experience with them. My classmate, Fr. Nick, and I went to their convent early in the morning and the sister who was met us was smiling from ear to ear. She greeted us with such joy and took us into the chapel so we could celebrate Mass. As we were in the midst of Mass, the nuns knelt the whole time on the wooden floor. They had two chairs in the chapel for the priests, because we are weak, but the nuns knelt the whole Mass. Fr. Nick was the main celebrant and I was the concelebrant. He read the gospel and began preaching. When he was preaching, he talked about God's word, of course, but then he made fun of me (Can you imagine? He made fun of the way I talk, of my Pittsburgh dialect! He is going to purgatory for a long time!) You know what those nuns were doing as he made fun of me? They were laughing hysterically, bent over, on their knees! The surest sign of God's presence in someone's life is joy. If there is no joy then we are not living the will of God. We must be people of Joy.

Now joy and humor are not always the same thing. Once I was speaking at a young adult conference, and I was picking on one of the priests who was with me. Everyone was laughing. The priest I picked on did not laugh at all. Afterward I said, "Father, you weren't laughing when I was picking on you." And he responded, "I wasn't going to say anything unless you brought it up." Then he said, "You have a negative humor."

I said, "I know, that is part of my personality."

He said, "Don't you think that is wrong?" (I thought, "Well, no, up until now no one has ever said anything about it to me.") He continued, "I don't think it is of God." I promised that I wouldn't use any more negative humor for the rest of the weekend. He complained, "Just the rest of the weekend? How about the rest of your life!" (Oh dear, have mercy.)

Now, negative humor is usually a guy thing. We pick on one another. Trust me, when priests get together there is a lot of negative humor. I usually don't use it if I know people are sensitive, but I don't think it is evil! My point is that people have different kinds of humor, but joy is a different thing.

Too many people, in my opinion, have taken the joy out of following Christ. We make Christianity humorless. Jesus said He wants your joy to be complete! Are you a person of joy?

Once when I was talking with a fellow priest, we got into a bit of a debate. His whole point was that we must suffer a lot before we die. I said, "Oh, I don't buy that at all. If this God of the Universe just wants us to suffer for suffering sake, I don't believe it."

He said, "Well, when one of us dies then we will find out what is really true."

So I said, "If it is really true that God wants us to suffer for suffering sake, He is not love. I believe that there is suffering on earth, but it is a suffering of love. When I give up my life for you, I am going to suffer. But it is a joyful suffering because something better is coming out of it."

Suffering in itself stinks! What you do when you are suffering is offer it up for somebody else. Then your act becomes an act of love. In Luke 4:38–39, we see that one of the very first miracles Jesus performed was to heal St. Peter's mother-in-law. What did she do right after she was healed? She served, or you might say that she loved.

When Jesus touched someone, there was healing, not suffering. That is the reality when you read the Word of God. Jesus brought healing. Jesus took dead people and brought them back to life. Jesus touched the only son of a mother and brought him back to life (see Luke 7:1–15). Jesus always brings healing and life.

You can have any perspective you want, but I would rather have the perspective of a God who wants to heal me and bring me back to life than a God who enjoys my suffering. Think about it. God wants you to be joyful. That is God's will for you. If you are going to live the will of God, you and I should have joy in our lives. If there is no joy in your life, why not? It is not God's will for you to be joyless. He wants you to have joy. So why don't you have it?

Some people think we are just supposed to suffer on earth. No, that's absolutely wrong. That is not what Jesus Christ said. He did say, *In the world you will have trouble* (see John 16:33), but the trouble is not from Him. It is from the world. After Jesus tells us we will have trouble, He immediately adds, *But have courage, I have overcome the world.*

Throughout my years as a priest, I have been an instrument of God to people as they are dying. I have been able to anoint people, give them the Last Rites of the Church, and be with them to get them ready to go home to God. Often after I have anointed someone, I say the Divine Mercy Chaplet. As I say, "Have mercy on us and on the whole world," I put the person's name into the prayer to personalize it for them. For example, "Have mercy on Alice and on the whole world." As I pray with them, I reflect on the fact that soon they will see Jesus face-to-face. I always tell them, "Don't be afraid. He loves you more than anyone on this earth. He is waiting. You are going home!"

When you know that you are going to go home to Jesus, it should not cause you fear. It should bring you great joy. Now that rite of passage will be different for all of us, but we have to make sure we are all on the same page when it comes to this — it is God's will for you to be with Him in heaven. Is it your will?

God does not want you in purgatory. You might end up there, but He does not want you there. So how can you go right to heaven and be with God? By receiving the last rites. That is why it is always a good idea to pray to St. Joseph for a happy death because if you die with the last rites, you make a good confession, you are anointed, you receive Viaticum, and then you get something quite interesting — at that moment, the Church gives you a plenary indulgence. A plenary indulgence takes care of the temporal punishment due all confessed sin. That is your ticket to get right into heaven. By the grace of Christ, who died on the cross for you, He gives heaven completely to you.

If you and I go to heaven, it is not because of what we did; it is because how we cooperated with what Jesus did for us. Who was the first to get to heaven next to Jesus Christ? The Good Thief. He was bad his whole miserable life. Right before he died he looked at the God of the Universe and said, *Jesus, remember me when you come into your kingdom* (see Luke 23:42). His will and Christ's will at that moment became one. He was saved by the grace of God. *Jesus assured him: Today you will be with me in paradise!* (see Luke 23:43). Jesus didn't say "next week," or "after 50 years," or "at the end of time." He said *today!*

God wants you to be with Him as much as He wanted the good thief to be with Him, so do not be afraid. Live every day as if it was your last. Love Him with all that you are, and desire

Him with your whole being. He will fulfill your desire forever with the gift of Himself if you trust Him, so trust Him!

When Jesus comes at the end of time, some people will see His face and scream and run away. Other people will see the face of Jesus and smile with joy from ear to ear. It all depends on us. Do we love Him? Are we ready for Him to come? Or are we afraid of Him and going to run away? I hope that we all love Him and want for Him to come. Aren't you excited? I don't know how excited He is going to be, but we should be extremely excited because this is what we were created for.

Some people take Christianity and twist it around to fit their own little beliefs. Throughout the centuries, people have taken Christianity and put their own little spin on it. They take the joy out of Christianity. Many heresies have arisen which, for a time, have turned people away from the true Faith and the true teaching of the Church. I always tell people "Focus on the teaching of the Church, and focus on the teachings of the Scriptures and you will never go wrong." Everything else is projection and people's opinion, and I am not the least bit interested in it. We need to focus on what is true, and what has been revealed to us.

Remember, we have the four modern marks of the Church today: one, holy, catholic, and apostolic. The original four marks of the Church are exclaimed in Acts 2:42: *They devoted themselves to the teaching of the apostles, the communal life, to the breaking of the bread, to the prayers.* These are the four marks of the early Church. If we are going to live in God's will, we have to do the same types of things as the early Church. *As it was in the beginning, is now, and will be forever.*

We have to be people who dedicate ourselves to the teachings of the Church. Isn't this amazing? It does not say that the early Christians devoted themselves to "the Word of God," but *to the teaching of* the Word of God from *the apostles.* What were the apostles teaching? The Word of God. But they taught it the way Jesus taught it — with authority.

This is the problem. You have some people and churches that proclaim God hates people, and then they say they are preaching God's will. But they are wrong. They are evil. Satan gets into people, takes the Word of God and twists it until they believe what he wants them to believe instead of what God revealed. Just because you quote Scripture does not mean you are of God. The devil quotes Scripture all the time. Satan took the Word of God and quoted it to Jesus (who was the Word) and tried to twist it to have Jesus do what he wanted.

Who are the apostles today? The bishops. If you are teaching according to the apostles then you must teach according to the magisterium of the Church, which will keep you in the will of God. This is the official teaching of the Church — not ideas from different people who have their own interpretations.

One more thing: We are not just limited to Scripture in the Catholic Church. Tradition is more than just Scripture — and has been right from the beginning. If someone tries to tell you something that it is not in the official Catholic teaching, then say that you are not the least bit interested in their opinion. The truth is not your interpretation. Truth is what God has proclaimed through the Church. Give me the truth.

When you go to the *Catechism of the Catholic Church*, the opening line by Blessed Pope John Paul the Great, with emphasis, says: "GUARDING THE DEPOSIT OF FAITH IS THE MISSION WHICH THE LORD ENTRUSTED TO HIS CHURCH, and which she fulfills in every age." Guarding the deposit of the faith is the mission entrusted by Christ to His Church. Not love one another. Not that there is a Trinity. The deposit of the faith is everything the Church teaches — that God is a Trinity, that God is love, that Jesus is God, that we are saved by grace, that God asks us to love one another! The main job of the Church is to guard and protect revelation. When you start messing with revelation, you mess with truth. You have to guard this tradition, this revelation, because that is what is most important. The early Church dedicated itself to listening to the tradition of the apostles, which was given to them by the revelation of God Himself. Remember when Peter proclaims that Jesus is the Messiah? Jesus says, *No mere man has revealed this to you, but my heavenly Father.* Then He declares that Peter is *rock* and gives him the keys to heaven (see Matthew:17–18).

The second mark of the early Church was they *devote themselves to the communal life.* There are no Lone Rangers in Christianity. We always come together as a community. That is why you can't just stay home on Sunday and talk to God while lying in your bed, or go out into the woods and commune with God. You can do those things, yes, but God calls you to be a member of the family. It is as if you would talk to your father about the rule that says you have to come and eat dinner with the family every Sunday. You might not like the rule and even say you aren't going to do it, but your father would look at you and say, "Excuse me, if you love me, you love the family. You are going to come home and have dinner with the family once a week. You are a member of the family." God does the same thing. He says, "I want you to come home and I want you to have dinner with your family at least once a week." The Church is your family and we need to come together and eat as a family.

What do you think heaven is going to be? Do you think when you drop dead that you are just going to stare at God forever? I don't want to go if that is what heaven is like. After a couple of million years, I think I would get bored. Heaven is a community where God loves us and we love Him and we love one another forever. As we talked about before, there is no communion of the damned. If you go to hell, God forbid that anyone does, you are alone forever.

One of the experiences that converted St. Teresa of Ávila was God's revelation to her of hell. She said that she could not move. Her whole body was burning. All she could do was see other people burning in the same way, but she could not communicate with them. It was utter aloneness, forever.

Billy Joel was lying when he sang, "I'd rather laugh with the sinners than cry with the saints." That's a lie. The saints have joy forever. It is the communion of saints. We get to be forever together. When we have communion on earth, we already experience a taste of the communion of heaven.

Communion with Jesus is communion also with one another. Right now you are in communion with the Church Militant, with the Church Suffering in purgatory, and with the Church Triumphant. We are all one body. When you and I receive Jesus in the Eucharist, we have communion with Jesus and communion with one another.

Let's say you have someone you love in another part of the country. You may feel very far from them, but when you go to Communion on Sunday, and they go to Communion on Sunday you become one intimately with them. If you have a mother or father who has died, when you go to Communion you have union with them. That is what we mean when we say the early Church dedicated itself to the communal life. Communion is union.

This leads us to the fourth mark of the early Church, *the breaking of the bread*. The breaking of the bread is what they called the Eucharist. The communal life is best expressed in the Mass and the Eucharist. We use the sacraments to help us stay in the will of God, and going to Mass must become a habit in our lives. If the early Church had to do it, so must we. Every Mass is a living Sacrifice. Jesus who is alive is offering His life in sacrifice. When you and I join our lives with His in the Eucharist, we are offering our own lives as a living sacrifice. If we are dedicating ourselves to the breaking of the bread the way the early Church did, we become one with Jesus and one another.

All this comes down to the last practice that the early Church dedicated itself to, and what I have talked about throughout this book: prayer. The number one practice that will keep us in the will of God is prayer. There is no other way. We have to stay in prayer every day. As Paul would say, *Pray always* (see 1 Thess 5:17). Pray always.

There are many ways to do that. One of the oldest ways is the "Jesus Prayer" — "Lord, Jesus Christ, Son of the Living God, have mercy on me, a sinner." It becomes a part of your breath. As you breathe in you say, "Lord, Jesus Christ." As you breathe out, you say, "Son of the Living God." You breathe in again and say, "have mercy on me." You breathe out and say, "a sinner." This is an ancient practice in the Eastern Orthodox Church. Members used to carry long rosaries, also called "prayer ropes," and on every bead they would say, "Lord, Jesus Christ, Son of the Living God, have mercy on me, a sinner," so it became part of their breath. That is how they woke up. That is how they went to bed. They would say thousands and thousands of them.

Another way to pray always, and one of the ways I do it, is to try is to focus on a word that will instantly bring you into the presence of God. For me that word is *"abba,"* which means "Father," or "Daddy." When I say *"abba,"* I instantly come into the presence of my Father in heaven. Every one of us needs to find a word to help us to come into the ultimate reality, a word that will take you into the very presence of God, that will remind you, get you refocused to be with Him, and spend time with Him.

In summary, dedicate yourself to the teachings of the Church, to being a loving member of the Church community, to being dedicated to the Eucharist, and to being a person of prayer.

The common theme I hope you take away from this book is that there is no magical way to discern God's will. Knowing

God's will comes from living in a relationship with Jesus, and this relationship begins when you surrender your life completely to Him. Hopefully, you have fully surrendered yourself to the Lord. If not, before you end this book, you must do it or you will have wasted your time.

To make sure that you surrender to the Lord, I want to tell a story that I tell at the end of all my retreats and missions. It is the story of "The Man from Crete."

Crete is a little island off the coast of Greece. There once was a man who loved Crete. He worked the grapes of Crete, the olives trees of Crete. Every time a baby was born, he would be the first one there to kiss the baby. And when someone would die, he would be the first one there to offer his condolences.

He loved the land of Crete and all of the people of the land loved him. When he was 99 years old, it was time for him to die. Originally he only had sons, but so many women got on my case that I gave the ninety-nine-year-old guy a four-year-old daughter. So here he is with his daughter, his ten sons, his grandkids, his great-grandkids and he says, "Listen, it is time for me to die. I want you to take me out and lay me on my beloved Crete. I want to feel the sun once more on my face." And so, like good Catholic children, they obeyed.

They took him out and laid him on the land of Crete. He could feel the sun beating down on his face. He could feel the air go through his hair. He was so happy. He looked around at all his friends and relatives, his grandkids and his sons and his daughter, and he was so happy. Then he took a handful of the dirt of Crete and thought, "This is a symbol of everything I ever loved," and he closed his eyes and died.

When he opened his eyes again, he was before the pearly gates of heaven (and they really are pearly, don't you know), but he couldn't see in. Suddenly, the gates open up and God comes out dressed in long, black judgment robes.

He said, "Old man, you have loved me, and you have loved others. Come on home and enjoy eternal life." The old man gets up and starts walking toward those pearly gates. Then God looks over at him and asks, "What is that in your hand?"

The old man says, "It is Crete. It is a symbol of everything I have ever loved. It is all I have left of Crete."

God looks at him and says, "Sorry, no dirty hands in heaven. You are going to have to let it go."

The old man says, "I can't let go of this."

God says, "You must let go of it if you are going to come into the kingdom with me." And the old man says, "I can't. I will not let go of this. I can't."

God says, "Okay, it is your will. I love you. You can keep what you want, but you cannot enter." The man sat there on the curb outside of heaven holding onto his Crete as God walked sadly into the gates of heaven and the gates of heaven closed behind him.

God is a very persistent God, so the gates of heaven open after a couple of days and God comes out as a Bavarian beer-meister. He's wearing high socks, knickers, and suspenders. He even has one of those Oktoberfest hats with the feather in it and a big beer stein filled with German beer. He is singing, "Ya, ya, ya, ya," and says, "Old man, we are having a party and it is for you. Come on home and enjoy eternal life."

The old man asks, "Can I bring my Crete?"

God says, "No, I'm sorry. You can't bring your Crete."

Then the old man says, "Well then I'm not coming."

God says, "Fine, go to hell." (No, He didn't really, but He is the only one who could say that, isn't he?) So God walks sadly back through the gates of heaven and the gates of heaven close again.

Now I don't know if you have ever held on to dirt for any length of time, but imagine this man desperately holding on to this dirt. All of the moisture is going out of it and it is becoming like sand. It is sifting through his fingers and he is trying desperately to hold on to the grains. Finally the gates of heaven open one last time. God comes out as the little boy Jesus, no more than three or four years old. Jesus comes over and says, "Whatcha doin?"

The old man says, "Let me go. How dare you call yourself a God of love? If you were a God of love, you would not ask me to give up the only thing I have left. This is everything I have ever loved. If you were a God of love you wouldn't ask me to give up everything."

Jesus just looked at him and said, "Old man, that just looks like a bunch of dirt to me. Old man, let the dust go to the wind. Grab my hand and come home."

The old man thinks about how desperately he is holding on to this dust that was going through his fingers and how hard he is trying to hold onto it. Finally, he opens his hand, and the wind, the breath, the *ruah* of God, the spirit of the Living God, comes and blows away everything he had been holding.

With an empty hand and great sadness, he bends down and takes the boy Jesus' hand. As he takes the hand of Christ, which is the only way to get to heaven, Christ leads him into the kingdom of heaven. The gates of heaven close behind him, and the old man is sad as he thinks about all the things he gave up. Suddenly he looks up and starts to laugh because what is before him? All of Crete! Everything he ever loved, everything he ever wanted is there for him.

What is it you hold on to so tightly that you cannot surrender it to receive everything God wants to give you? What do you want? Remember that with God you have everything. Without God you have nothing but a handful of dirt.

Every year on Ash Wednesday, we are told, "Remember, man, that you are dust and unto dust you shall return." You are going to die. You are going to become dust, some of you faster than others because you are going to be cremated. But I promise you, every one of you will become dust. You can stay dust forever or you can surrender your dust and life to Jesus Christ and He will take your life and give you His.

Christ is right here with you. This isn't some magic. It is true reality. Christ asks you now, "I have given everything for love of you. Will you give everything for love of me?

If you have never fully surrendered your life totally to Jesus Christ, you cannot end this book until you do. Just pray this prayer with all your heart, surrender yourself to Him now, forever. He is waiting.

> Lord, Jesus Christ, I acknowledge that I am a sinner. I am sorry for my sins. And I beg you to forgive me. Come into my heart. Take control of my life, be my Lord and Savior. Fill me with your Holy Spirit and make me your disciple. I love you, Lord Jesus Christ, and I surrender my life to you forever. Amen.

And now it begins.

Steps to Surrendering Your Life

1. Decide to live a life of joy!
2. Be a living sacrifice.
3. Meditate on John 15:9. Let it penetrate your whole being.
4. Find a word that will bring you instantly into an awareness of God's presence.
5. Dedicate yourself to the teaching of the Church, to being a loving member of the Church community, to being dedicated to the Eucharist, and being a person of prayer.
6. Surrender everything to Jesus Christ!

A Prayer to Help You on Your Way

Prayer for Discernment[5]

My Lord God, I have no idea where I am going.

I do not see the road ahead of me. I cannot know for certain where it will end.

Nor do I really know myself, and the fact that I think I am following your will does not mean that I am actually doing so.

But I believe that the desire to please you does in fact please you and I hope that I have that desire in all that I am doing.

And I know that if I do this, you will lead me by the right road although I may know nothing about it.

Therefore will I trust you always though I may seem to be lost and in the shadow of death, I will not fear, for you are ever with me and you will never leave me to face my perils alone.

Amen.

— Thomas Merton

ENDNOTES

1. Fr. James Geoghegan, O.C.D., "The Parents of St. Thérèse," *The Proceedings of the Second Regional Congress, Discalced Carmelite Third Order* (1974): accessed March 2011, www.thereseoflisieux.org/the-parents-of-st-therese-fr.

2. www.catholic.org/saints/saint.php?saint_id=65.

3. Egan, Eileen, and Bauer, Judy, *At Prayer with Mother Teresa* (Liguori, MO: Liguori Press, 1995), p. 101.

4. If you want help with this, you can purchase my CD or DVD entitled "Prayer," which is available through my foundation at www.thereasonforourhope.org. In this CD/DVD, I actually walk you through this prayer experience.

5. Adapted from Thomas Merton's Prayer for Discernment (www.discernmentresources.blogspot.com/2009/02/thomas-mertons-prayer-for-discernment.html).